SUMMERLANDISH
DO AS I SAY, NOT AS I DID

Summer Land

hardie grant books

MELBOURNE · LONDON

Published in 2013 by Hardie Grant Books

Hardie Grant Books (Australia)
Ground Floor, Building 1
658 Church Street
Richmond, Victoria 3121
www.hardiegrant.com.au

Hardie Grant Books (UK)
Dudley House, North Suite
34–35 Southampton Street
London WC2E 7HF
www.hardiegrant.co.uk

Cataloguing in publication data is available from the National Library
of Australia

Summerlandish: Do as I say, not as I did
ISBN 978 1 7427 06443

Cover design by Luke Lucas
Author photographs by Henryk Lobaczewski
Text design by Kinart
Typeset in Olympian 9.6/15pt by Cannon Typesetting
Printed and bound in Australia by Griffin Press

For Paul & Donna
(my two #1s)

Some names
have been
changed to
protect the
guilty. Some
haven't.

CONTENTS

PROLOGUE

It was a resplendent day in the outback when my friends and I set out to experience the famous Bell Gorge, known for its daunting cliffs and occasional crocodiles. To get there, we had to drive off-road for an hour, wade through unpleasantly croc-infested water and hike for miles. If you were brave enough to attempt 'The Jump', though, you had to climb even higher on the extremely rocky terrain that stretched over the gorge. The men in my group were anxious to race each other to the top and be the first to conquer the mammoth cliff.

The girls and I laid down our towels and waved goodbye as the guys set off in search of bigger thrills. (I don't see what could be a bigger thrill than achieving the ultimate cinnamon glow, but whatever.) Before we knew it, the guys were at the top of the cliff, a little more than 50 feet above us. Expecting the men to jump right away, we all had our cameras ready and waiting. And waiting. And waiting … What was the hold-up?

The boys were simply standing still at the top. It appeared that they were trying to figure out the best angle, and what trees and rocks they needed to clear. Naturally, I started getting antsy. Why didn't they just jump? I was once too afraid go on a massive water slide at Jekyll Island's Summer Waves Water Park in Georgia, at age seven, and have regretted it ever since. From then on, I've always faced my fears.

Suddenly, I heard myself make some asinine comment about the guys being too scared, and proclaimed that I was going to make the jump myself. After checking to be sure that my pale-purple string bikini was double-knotted, I set off for the summit.

When I reached the peak, the sickening realisation set in that we were a lot higher than it looked from down below. The girls looked like ants. But there was no turning back now.[1] The next chain of events happened in less than thirty seconds: I quickly asked where to jump; Rob, a rough-around-the-edges English bloke, pointed to the left; I immediately proceeded to hurl my body over the edge, dropping 50 feet.

It felt like I was plummeting for a solid two minutes. I even had time to make eye contact with a bird and contemplate how painful my imminent death would be. And then, travelling at the speed of light, I hit the water ... with my legs open. The water rushed into my anus like it was trying to capsize the *Titanic*. My organs felt like they were drowning, and I couldn't kick my legs.

I tried to yell for help, but had gotten the wind completely knocked out of me by the less-than-graceful landing. After I dog paddled to shore, my friends managed to pull me

---

1   I feel like many of the rules from *Wedding Crashers* apply in life, especially rule #76: 'No excuses; play like a champion.'

out of the water and drag me onto dry land. Emily, my bestie from university, then helped me crawl behind a rock where, with my swimsuit pulled to the side, I immediately shat and peed out of my ass. It was like the enema from hell. The only thing that calmed me was the fact that Gwyneth Paltrow would probably endorse it as a kind of natural colonic.

Emily was laughing hysterically, because a group of perfectly sculpted Australian men noticed what was happening and were pointing at me. Feeling somewhat embarrassed, I did my best to tidy myself up with leaves and hide my pile of watery sewage with some dirt. Finally relieved, I stood up and limped to the rest of my friends. They informed me that the whole thing had been caught on video, which instantly made the entire experience (watery faeces and all) totally worth it.

The guys, still up at the top, now had no choice but to do their jumps. It wasn't only that some girl had just stolen their thunder; it was that some *American* girl had just stolen their thunder. For SHAME. So they finally took the leap. (Followers.) Afterwards, we all gathered to talk about the thrill and the height, and to compare our war wounds. Rob's tailbone was throbbing, and another guy's foot was black and blue. It was obvious that we were all hurting, but I secretly felt like I had internal injuries (and I was pretty sure that approximately two feet of my intestines were hanging out of my butt).

I tried to giggle with my friends, but it felt like the shattered pieces of my tailbone were individually stabbing my already-damaged internal organs. A bit later, Rob came up and whispered to me, 'Miss, have you got your period?' At this point, being a thousand per cent confident that I was *not* on my period, I realised that blood was probably seeping out of my ass.

I remained outwardly calm, but in reality I was wondering where, exactly, the laceration was: on the inside, or the puckered part? Unfortunately, I was definitely *not* in a position to sit down with a hand mirror and survey the damage. Laughter about my butthole injury ensued from every person in our group. And not just your standard 'ha ha', but actual German laughs followed by (in an extremely thick accent), 'It was sofa king funnyyyy!' And the English of course yelled, 'You have a bloody arsehole! Literally!'

We eventually made it to the car, where I quickly learned that I would not be able to sit for a very long time. Instead, I had to lie across the back seat and practise Lamaze breathing as the car made its way over the corrugated roads. (It felt much more like Mr Toad's Wild Ride than it had on the way there.) Rob did his best to avoid potholes, but the corrugated roads made it impossible for me to unclench.

After what seemed like forever we stopped at a roadhouse, where I immediately used a payphone to call my mom, Donna, in America and tell her about my self-inflicted injury. She scared the shit out of me (no pun intended) when she told me that, if there was poop in the wound, I could get a nasty infection.

Next, I called my lover, Paul. I explained in detail that we would probably never be able to try anal sex again. Then I hung up and got Emily to come back to the car with me. Yes, I made her look. We spread my ass cheeks and she informed me that I had split the top of my anus. The cut was about an inch long and stretched from my poop chute to my tailbone. The good news: it wasn't very deep. (I tried to get her to take pictures, but the flash washed out my butthole.)

Over the next several days I obsessively applied disinfectant to my injury and did my best not to wipe poop into it, and eventually my flesh wound was fully healed. However, my tailbone continued to turn every shade of purple for the next two weeks. (I feel like getting multiple enemas after eating curry for ten days straight, in Calcutta, would have been less detrimental to me.) Whenever I was in the shower, I checked with my hands to make sure my bowels were all still tucked up neatly inside. I had watched plenty of health shows and knew that I was in no mood for haemorrhoids.

The stress of trying to heal my injury started to weigh on me. When I looked at my friends' lives back in America on Facebook, they looked so clean, so successful and so happy. I was living in a tent, trying to avoid piles, battling thrush, living off cans of tuna and really starting to miss my family. How had I gotten here? Why had I *needed* to jump off that cliff?

LET ME TELL YOU ABOUT DONNA

Donna is a sister, daughter, friend, widow, aunt, cousin, frat mom, garden club member, former blonde, former hypnotist, former preschool teacher and avid Facebooker.

Her hobbies include playing solitaire on her computer for hours at a time, walking with friends, and occasionally binge-eating a Costco-sized container of spearmint-flavoured mints. Donna, like most twenty-somethings in the 70s, used to love cocaine, cigarettes and sex, but since she's been sober for thirty years, her vices now are mainly food, social networking and real estate.

Even though (or perhaps because) Donna is not the best money manager, she's unbelievably generous. Need money for a car or that mortgage? Donna has your back! Need a meal? Donna knows all the best sushi and Mexican spots, and it's her treat. Need every Beanie Baby ever made? Donna is totally on board.

This 5'4" West Virginia–born beauty has transformed from cheerleader to wife to mother in the best way possible.

She thinks she's fat. But really, she's put on the perfect amount of weight for a proper 'mom hug'.

While in many ways she is the quintessential flower-child who radiates peace and love, she really likes the words 'fuck' and 'shit'. She's been Christian, Jewish and agnostic. She's been a vegetarian and a carnivore. (I mean, you can't move to Florida and resist Zaxby's chicken. It's a Southern thing.) She's done yoga and meditation, and participated in drum circles. She's been a member of the PTA and Hadassah, and has campaigned for Obama. Her favourite crafts include pottery and stained glass, but the thing about Donna is that when she gets good enough at whatever she's doing, she loses interest.

She's lived all over, loved a lot and always made people laugh. But, most importantly, Donna is my mom.

Gchat log, September 2010
Summer: Hi Mom! Our plane is delayed.
Donna: Hey Honey. I had breakfast with Lisa and she loves your writing. She said that you are an excellent writer, a very good storyteller and that she looks forward to each blog post.
Summer: YAY! Jeanne wrote me too. She likes it! However, I am scared about what will happen when she reads about vagina farts. lol 'Everybody vagina farts.'
Donna: I am pretty sure that I have never.
Summer: Liar.
Donna: Does it happen during sex because I can't really remember sex.
Summer: hahahahaa
Donna: I had a little poop come out one time during sex. This little tiny ball of poop lying there on the sheet.
Summer: Did he see????
Donna: We did acid for the first and only time that day and yes he did see. Maybe that's why my relationships never last.

NOW LET ME TELL YOU ABOUT ME

Most people say they don't remember birth, but not me. I recall almost every glorious, gooey moment. From the time Donna scheduled her C-section[1] to the minute the doctor wrapped his latex-covered hands around my fragile newborn rib cage, I remember it all. Even before I was lifted from my mother's gaping belly, I knew that my impending arrival on earth was going to be eventful. There were people to meet, actions to regret and many other learning experiences to be had.

Okay, fine, I admit it: I don't remember any of this. I do, however, remember looking at pictures of my birth at the ripe old age of three. I had just finished flipping through the very detailed illustrations in *The Joy of Sex* (clearly the shaved look wasn't popular yet) and scarred myself

---

1   She scheduled a C-section because an astrologist had told her that even though I was due on the 22nd of August, I should be born on the 21st because I would like her better.

with the graphic images of vaginas expanding to the size of manholes (everything looks bigger when you're a kid) in *A Child Is Born*. (Why Donna thought these were appropriate 'bottom shelf' books is beyond me.) Finally, I crawled over to our 'Precious Memories' albums to discover the beautiful, bloody photographic essay of my own entrance into the world. Even though my dad, Steve, had passed away just nine weeks and six days before my birth, these pictures showed a beautiful new family. My favourite was a group shot of Donna, my two-year-old brother, Brett, and me.

The man missing from the pictures deserves a whole book to himself, but I will tell you this: he was a Jewish jeweller who served with the Marines in the Vietnam War, and he had more charisma buried in his chest hair (along with multiple gold chains) than anyone else in the 80s had in their entire bodies. He was fun. A lot of fun. One story my Uncle John John (not really my uncle; not really 'John John' on his birth certificate, either) likes to tell me is about the time my dad decided to turn his VW bug into a convertible. With a chisel and a hammer.

Sadly, alcohol, valium and marijuana got the best of him early one morning when he went swimming in the Atlantic Ocean and drowned. His body washed up onshore at Pawleys Island, South Carolina, and was found by a jogger.

Amazingly, Donna never let us feel the void of not having a father. She just explained that Dad's body was broken and he couldn't use it anymore, but he was probably watching over us from heaven.

Some might say that, even with all that love, my childhood (and adulthood) has been a bumpy ride. Although most kids would like to blame their parents for their issues or 'mishaps' in life, I have no one to point the finger at but myself. Growing up without my father definitely gave me some 'daddy issues', but I certainly feel like Donna made up for that tenfold. Granted, when I was in her womb, she chain-smoked, ate raw ground beef saturated in Worcestershire sauce and consumed a fair amount of caffeine. But it was probably difficult to find a pregnant woman in the 80s who didn't pop open a nice cold can of Tab or spark up a Virginia Slim.[2]

No, it wasn't her prenatal behaviour that contributed to my outlandish life. In fact, I was born healthy and given every opportunity in the world. The problems arose when I began taking *literally* every opportunity as it popped up. Like the opportunity to get a fake ID at fourteen, or a zodiac tattoo at sixteen. But I think I'm getting ahead of myself. As Maria once said, 'Let's start at the very beginning, a very good place to start.'

---

2 I would like to point out that, at one point in time, doctors used leeches to suck out sickness. Donna just took one for the team and learned by experience. (Well, really *I* took one for the team and lucked out by not being born too brain dead.)

LESSONS LEARNT
AS A KID

When I was almost one, Donna took us to visit her cousin Hido in Gainesville, Florida. Boy, was she blown away. Gainesville had a major university, a domestic airport and more playgrounds than a single mother with two hyperactive kids could ever dream of. The second afternoon of our visit, we were all cruising around and looking at houses (because this was and still is one of Donna's favourite things to do). Eventually we pulled in to the beautiful Rock Creek subdivision. The houses were all single-storey ranch homes with lovely yards. There was a neighbourhood playground and pool, and tennis courts! There was also a 'For Sale' sign in front of one of the houses.

Donna smiled and said, 'Let's just knock and see if we can take a look around.'

We went in and met a lovely family. Donna fell in love with the back deck and, because Donna is Donna, she bought the house right then. (This was the first of more than a few large impulse purchases.) With the paperwork in motion, we went back to West Virginia, loaded up the Cadillac Sedan de Ville and headed south. My dad's mom, Gladys, drove the car; Brett, Mom and I took a plane.

The thing about Gainesville is that it's located in north-central Florida. Most people think Miami when they think of Florida, but I need you to think *True Blood*, backwoods, 'I ♥ Jesus and football' Florida. No-beach Florida. It was an amazing place to grow up, but it definitely had its share of rednecks. (Since Donna was from West Virginia, I don't think she noticed.)

Do: Wear underwear.

Not only had we moved to Florida, I had moved into Little Girl World. In case you don't know, it's that magical age (roughly two to five) where little girls have absolutely no idea what is going on and yet are having the best time of their lives, usually involving floral dresses, public settings and that little-girl shriek that only dogs can hear. This magical time of life is filled with child leashes, singalongs and trips to Disney World. If Little Girl World had a school play, it would be one in which the little girls just pick their noses and roll around on the stage, laughing. And when the curtain rises, they receive a deafening roar of *Awwww*s from a glowing sea of camcorders.

In Summer's World, I would throw my dress above my head, exposing my pair of minuscule, mosquito-bite nips and the fact that I'd chosen not to wear any underwear. And this would all happen as I twirled around in the checkout line of the Pic 'N' Save with my mom. After Donna's many efforts to provide me with every pair of Disney princess print or day-of-the-week underwear she could find, she finally hit a home run with a beautiful ruffled pair. Only one problem: the ruffles were on the back. That was simply not going to work for me; if I was going to wear underwear, I wanted to reap the benefits. So I started wearing them backwards, in order to get a good view of the pretty part. (It's important to love yourself first. If you feel good about you, other people will too.)

The fact that I was finally willing to wear undies was a step closer to domesticating little Summer, but I still tended to 'forget' them often. In preschool, we had a craft day that allowed us to go from station to station, trying unusual painting techniques. When it came time for me to use my feet to paint, I was abruptly stopped by my teacher and told that I could no longer participate in that particular activity. Confused and disappointed, I asked why. It turned out that it was because I was wearing a dress and had no underwear on. When I placed the paintbrush between my toes and stretched my legs out to meet the easel, my vagina was on show and, apparently, flashing your hoo-ha at school is generally discouraged. I remember being embarrassed for a nanosecond, and then skipping off back into Little Girl World to chew on some earthworms.

Unfortunately, that was not the first (or the last) time that my lack of underwear affected my day-to-day life. Once, after swim time at summer camp, I decided that I needed to do something about my wet shirt and undies. I came up with the perfect solution: just don't wear them! And, with that problem solved, I stepped into my semi-dry overalls and snapped a clip over each nipple. I thought it looked awesome, since each brass hook framed an areola almost perfectly. When I got to my drama elective and ran on stage, my counsellor, Laurel, came up to me and started examining my attire. She then gently said, 'Today is an underwear *and* shirt day,' which only mildly broke my spirit.

Of course, Little Girl World is a bittersweet place, because your time there is limited. Eventually, you grow a conscience and start learning the rules of society. My exit happened when I was five. I had developed a harmless crush on one of the instructors at my brother's taekwondo studio. His name was Mark. My name was Smitten. Not really knowing how to show my feelings to this boy, I decided to dedicate every arts and crafts project I ever made to him. One day I worked until my fingers were raw on a cross-stitching of our future house with the words 'Home Sweet Home' on it. (I wanted him to know that I was a provider.)

Our relationship showed so much promise. He made me laugh, I made him Fimo beads[1]. Everything was perfect. That is, until the summer of 1992. Donna and I were at the studio to pick up Brett. In an effort to look good for Mark, I was wearing one of my most beautiful party dresses and some Sam & Libby slip-ons with fetching bows on the toes. I had just finished constructing a particularly challenging birdhouse and could not wait to show him. He loved it, of course, and lifted me off the ground for a hug. As he held me, my dress got caught on his forearm and slid up above my butt. Within two seconds, my fear was confirmed: I was, in no way, shape or form, wearing any underwear

---

1   Fimo beads are the bomb. You make them out of polymer clay and then bake them. It's
     totally beading–meets–Easy Bake Oven. Basically, this gift was beyond thoughtful.

that day. Both of my cheeks clenched as the entire studio saw my full moon.

Quickly, I squirmed out of Mark's grasp and attempted to clothe myself. Then I stood still, thinking about my exposure. (My mind flashed to the decision I had made that morning to leave my ruffled pair in the drawer.) I was officially embarrassed, and the feeling was *not* going away. That was when I knew it: Little Girl World was gone for good. My carefree innocence had been stripped from me, and now it was as absent as my undies. When I think back to that magical time, it seems like there are really only two things that can pull one out of it: it's either love or public humiliation. And sometimes, it's both.

Do:
Dig through your poop.

Growing up in Gainesville, Brett liked to ask Donna if we could get a new dad and name him Steve. As for four-year-old me, without a father figure I started turning to Brett for a male role model. I followed him *everywhere* and mimicked *everything* that he deemed cool. If he slept in Ghostbusters sheets, I slept in Ghostbusters sheets. If he decided to watch *Beavis and Butthead*, I would watch them too (and act like them in public, which tended to mortify my mom).

I've since determined that the bond between my brother and me was my first abusive relationship. Donna says that I was born in love with him, but that he taught me to hate him. The more he would push me away and tell me I sucked, the more I wanted to be just like him and gain his affection.

Donna, Brett and I got into the habit of going to TCBY for frozen yoghurt. Fuelled by triple-decker parfaits, which were topped with sugary candy on top of sugary fruit on top of sugary whipped cream on top of sugary sugar, Brett and I would burst through our front door like Tasmanian devils on a methamphetamine bender. After changing into our white taekwondo uniforms and respective belts (for no apparent reason), we would chase each other around the house and backyard for hours (or until our beanbag chairs beckoned to us from their position in front of the TV, where we ate our nutritious, processed, frozen meat/potato/gelatin dinners, which *always* included my favourite: French fries).

One evening I was playing with a handful of coins, watching *Gremlins*, bending one of my brother's Transformers in every position possible to see if it had disappointing male parts like my Ken doll and, of course, eating French fries. (Donna probably wasn't aware at the time that toddlers could be heavily medicated for ADHD.) I was sprawled out on the floor, wrapping the fries around the edges of the coins to make circles because I was really into shapes at the time. In the midst of all the eating, making shapes, and asexual Transformers, I felt something go down my throat that did NOT feel like a fry. Wisely, I decided to count my change. Five cents short!

I ran to Donna to tell her that I'd swallowed a nickel and was going to die, and that she could have my collection of My Little Ponies and Lisa Frank stickers. She told me that I would live, and that it was going to come out my other end.

I was so excited!!! I couldn't wait to poop. The next day, I jumped out of bed like it was Christmas morning. (Christmas morning in our Jewish household always meant a trip to the Magic Kingdom at Disney.) I ran to the bathroom to let one out. With the door open, I yelled out to Donna, 'Come quick! I'm pooping!'

Donna showed up with a coathanger to poke around and see if the nickel had passed. After a quick peek, she found that IT HAD! The five-cent piece was promptly fished out and washed. I was proud of my well-travelled nickel, and asked my mom what we should do with it. She said we could put it in her special jewellery box, next to Brett's *Teenage Mutant Ninja Turtles* opening-day movie tickets, to have when I was older.

And Donna isn't one of those moms who say something just to make their child forget about it. No, that nickel is still there for me when I am mature enough to have it. I'm hoping I can get it any day now.

Don't: Underestimate the power of a psychic.

Life is full of ups and downs. Thankfully, Gainesville isn't a bad place to live. One of the many reasons is the annual Hogtown Medieval Fair. I swear I'm not exaggerating when I say that this event is in my Top Three Places To Go file.

(One being Disney World, duh. Two being the Medieval Fair. And three being Weeki Wachee, a magical place where mermaids exist. Seriously. They are real. Google it.) No matter what is going wrong in your world, whether you've just had your heart broken or you've seen Mickey Mouse with his mask off at Disney, the Medieval Fair will turn that frown upside down.

On the days that we were going to the Medieval Fair, we loaded ourselves into our white Dodge mini-van in record time. After a quick drive to the fairgrounds, we passed through the turnstiles and entered a world of jousting, food wagons, medieval weaponry and games. Musicians playing pan flutes serenaded our journey back in time to the Middle Ages. Countless humans, dressed in everything from tunics to chain mail to little horns and pointy princess hats, invited us to partake in a multitude of amazing events. These inexplicably included dipping our hands in wax, filling glass bottles with coloured sand (who knew sand was purple, green, blue, red and yellow back in the day?), and riding camels and elephants.

Brett got to work as a volunteer one year: he walked around selling little bags of hay to be spun into gold. I was insanely jealous and still am to this day. (We also went to a chain version of the Medieval Fair on steroids, Medieval Times, in Orlando, where a knight once threw Brett a rose after a jousting match. Brett's beautiful, shoulder-length blond hair always seemed to overshadow me. I literally choked with envy on the chicken I was eating and had to be given the Heimlich manoeuvre. Life was hard.)

On one particular day, after a noteworthily horrific Medieval Fair temper tantrum (I wanted a $75 quill pen and $50 ink to colour with), Donna needed some breathing room and peace. Naturally, she decided to drop me off at the palm reader. Perhaps she was hoping for a glimpse at a less psychotic future for her crazy (but adorable) daughter. As the all-knowing Ezmerelda (probably not her real name, but we'll go with it) gazed into my hand, I could tell right away that she knew her shit. This lady had the vision to look right past the grease from a giant medieval turkey leg and give me the most honest advice I had ever heard. She touched me right above my top lip and bluntly said, 'If you don't learn to control your temper, you're going to grow up to be a bitch.'

Do:
Pee when
you need to.

I completely understood her brutally honest statement. Ezmerelda was undoubtedly referring to my life up to that point, which, since I was transitioning out of Little Girl World, had been spent tearing my hair out in clumps, shrieking random sounds (which could have been mistaken for attempts to communicate with dolphins) and peeing on the floor. And the peeing part wasn't even out of necessity. I would just do it when I was really angry. Weird, right? I guess it started around the time I peed in my grandmother's shoes. 'That'll show Gladys ...' I thought as I sprayed her Ferragamo slingbacks.

Unfortunately, shoes weren't the only inanimate objects I liked to pee on. I once urinated in a plastic box that was used to hold flashcards. I don't remember if I was angry at the flashcards or just angry at the world, but I was constantly scared that someone would find (or smell) it. So I finally threw it away, ridding myself of the heavy burden of repeatedly trying to hide my pee box from friends and family.

Another urine event happened when Donna bought a cute little house that was built in the early nineteenth century. Unfortunately, there was only one bathroom and a tonne of work to be done on it. We began renovations by moving all of the furniture into the bathroom and bedrooms. The place looked like a mild episode of *Hoarders*, and there was really no convenient and private way to access the toilet. Anyway, I found myself home alone with a bunch of workmen who were refinishing our wood floors. Panicking because I unexpectedly had to urinate (really badly), I thought fast and remembered that the kitty litter had been moved to my bedroom. I clumsily stumbled over an ottoman, a chest of drawers, a box marked 'ugly mugs' and into my room. (Try stumbling over things when you urgently have to pee. It's not fun. Vaginas need zippers.)

When I finally made it, there was nothing else to do but squat over that kitty litter pan. As my pee shot out in full force, I inhaled the wonderful aroma of Arm & Hammer and totally understood why cats agree to use a tray full of tiny grey gravel as a toilet. After I was done, I looked down and knew from the size of the dark spot that this load was a doozy. Nothing a three-kilo cat could have done. I had to hide the evidence, and fast. Although the scooper nearly bent in half from the weight of my now-cemented pee, I managed to transport it across the cluttered room and dump it into a nearby Abercrombie & Fitch shopping bag. I buried it in the bottom of the garbage can in the kitchen, and Donna was none the wiser.

You're probably picturing five-year-old Summer peeing over a kitty litter tray, aren't you? Confession: I was nineteen when this happened.[2]

As I got older, it became less common for me to pee in places I shouldn't. (Except for the nineteen-year-old litter incident, and the twenty to thirty-five times I've drunk-peed in the street.) Another thing I got better at was remembering to wear underwear. Good thing, because I had much more important things to think about, such as ballet recitals and Halloween costumes.

My obsession with trying to be just like Brett was placed on hold, because next I became completely preoccupied with anything and everything to do with Hollywood. Like most children, I would get lost in movies, imagining I was bedknobbing broomsticks or flying around on enchanted floor coverings. And I wanted, more than anything, to dress

---

2   After my mom read this story, she looked at me seriously and admitted that she was always concerned about the fact that I would pee on the floor in fits of rage. She then confessed that one of our close family friends used to talk about a different child who would constantly urinate on her bedroom floor. Donna said that she could never bring herself to admit that her daughter was also a child who peed where she pleased. Guess the cat is out of the bag now. (Sorry, Mom. Maybe I'll take you to next year's Medieval Fair to make up for it.)

up as Tinker Bell and be strapped in a harness and fly from the top of Cinderella's Castle at Disney World. (Which is actually a real job and one that I still hope to get one day.)

But, unlike most children, I was allowed to watch any movie, no matter the content or rating. When I would hide my face from the image of Linda Blair spewing pea soup in *The Exorcist*, Donna would comfort me by pointing out the camera angles and special effects. Donna even gave me serious street cred at elementary school when she took me to see R-rated movie *The Crow* in 1994. (I was born in 1987. You do the math.) And this wasn't just some empty midweek matinee; this was opening night.

I should probably point out that my mom isn't some out-of-control, neglectful parent who is devoid of any emotion; she's quite the opposite, actually. Donna is just very honest and straightforward. Her 'parental guidance' could better be described as 'supportive suggesting'. I never had a curfew, could eat a bowl of frosting for breakfast if I wanted to and was allowed to go to school dressed as any of my favourite movie characters, if I so desired. (I always loved dressing like Vida from *To Wong Fu, Thanks for Everything, Julie Newmar*. You know – the transvestite played by Patrick Swayze.) She encouraged me to follow my wildest dreams and fully express myself, no matter how off-colour those ambitions and self-expressions happened to be. This, of course, included my dream of becoming a famous actress. I'm sure Donna must have thought that the unlimited variety of movies on hand would help me perfect my craft.

When I was in the third grade, I often played in Donna's closet. You could find anything in there, from blue leather cowboy boots to meditation crystals and Tarot cards. My favourite find was a tube top from her glory days. Of course, I put it on and wore it as a skirt. It went perfectly with the lace thong I would wedge up my butt and wrap over my shoulders. All together, I felt like I had created an outfit that was simply made to wear while enjoying the VHS tape of *Pretty Woman* for the thousandth time. (Found that tape in Donna's closet too. Turns out it was a Chanukah present for me.)

I worshipped Julia Roberts. She was beautiful, strong, yet, most importantly, a damsel in distress. ('Vivian from *Pretty Woman*' was always a severely underappreciated 'What do you want to be when you grow up?' response.) Never mind that she was selling her body for money and living in a sketchy apartment, she was a modern-day princess who needed to be saved.

When I accompanied my mom to Victoria's Secret one day, I imagined myself as Vivian: living in Beverly Hills, spending my nights sipping champagne and sitting on pianos, with Richard Gere standing firmly between my thighs. After some intense begging and pleading, Donna agreed to buy me a few pairs of lacy, sequined panties (better known as 'stripper-wear'). Once I had those, my after-school activities evolved from playing with my Barbie Dreamhouse to prancing around in my own dream world, with dollar bills tucked in my glittery underpants. And just like Vivian, I had no intention of kissing my make-believe clients on the mouth.

Around this time, I began to notice billboards on the interstate for something called Café Risqué. (I was an exceptional reader.) Donna explained that it was a strip club and restaurant, but that they did not serve alcohol because the girls got fully nude. (One of the many things I love about Donna is that she always takes the opportunity to educate and inform.) Donna said that the county commissioners thought that if they made it illegal to serve alcohol where there was nudity, then the owner of Café

Risqué would stop the nudity. They were wrong. The owner gave up the liquor licence instead: truck drivers shouldn't be drinking when they're going to be getting back on the road, anyway. This all seemed so exotic to me, so, naturally, as soon as we got home I stripped naked, donned my art smock as an apron and pretended that I was a waitress at Café Risqué. All good fun, until I decided to set up outdoor seating in the driveway.

Do: Approach Halloween like a pro.

The point is, if I could play dress-up for a living, I'd do it. So it should come as no surprise that Halloween has always been the most important day of the year for me. Born in August, I was probably the only two-month-old baby who did not fight the mandatory infant pumpkin attire on Halloween '87. And when I made it to third grade, my Halloween costume was a no-brainer. It was my chance to show the world my uncanny likeness to the twenty-something movie prostitute that I loved so dearly.

Seeking inspiration, I managed to find a trunk full of my brother's *Playboy* magazines. (I was really looking for cigarettes or bongs or anything else that might have gotten him into trouble, but got distracted by these beautiful women who were shamelessly posing in the buff.) A few were dressed as bunny rabbits. And since I was just as into small, fluffy animals as any other eight-year-old, my next oh-so-age-appropriate obsession was born. I simply had to be a Playboy bunny for Halloween. (Sorry, Julia.)

I convinced Donna to take me to the mall, where I had her purchase everything I'd need: boy shorts, a halter bikini top, detached cuffs complete with cufflinks, a bow tie, bunny ears, fishnet stockings (thank you, Spencer's[3]) and finally a pair of platform shoes covered with a sparkly black sandpaper-like material. (Still own these, they're sized for ants.) I could not wait to get to school so I could proudly walk across stage in the annual Halloween fashion show. I had a confidence about me that would put Paris Hilton to shame.

The big day finally came. All of the students, teachers and parents gathered in the Big Room and started munching on candy and lining up for the witch's brew (fruit juice served in a big cauldron with dry ice, so steam billowed out over the lip of the cauldron; it was pretty epic). With all of the kids vibrating on sugar highs, I lined up with my grade to go on stage. Once our class was called, I sauntered across the stage surrounded by my fellow classmates, who were dressed as hippies and Pink Ladies; in short, costumes that paled in comparison to mine.

What I was shocked to learn was that, apparently, an eight-year-old dressed as a Playboy bunny was *not* as glamorous to everyone else as it was to me. Most of my classmates didn't even know what I was. While I was explaining that I was an international sex symbol, I was simultaneously setting a school record for the highest number of outraged adults in the principal's office at once.

---

3   Spencer's is your go-to gift shop for inappropriate products available in children's sizes. Well, what I thought were children's sizes. Apparently, the 'fancy bra' I bought when I was six was actually a set of nipple pasties. Of course, as a child, this was my favourite shop.

When it came time to go trick-or-treating that night, I decided to change my costume. Not because of the criticism I'd received (they were all just jealous) but because I figured that, since I was going to be walking the streets that night, I should be a hooker. They *are* known as streetwalkers, after all. I carefully removed the animal accessories and traded my fluffy tail for a sexy training bra and cheerleading shorts. Once I topped it off with a feather boa, I was ready to hit the streets and get me some candy!

As a seasoned trick-or-treater, I knew to hit up the rich part of town. No point in wasting my time in the 'fun-size' neighbourhoods. I wanted me some KING-SIZED loot and Capri Suns. (Rich people loved giving out Capri Suns[4].) Plus, I knew these affluent neighbourhoods would appreciate my creative hooker costume.

(To answer your question, Social Services did not enter the picture until I was nine. And even then, it was only to verify that I'd broken my arm at school, and not at home. The fact that I was an aspiring prosti-tot with a glitter addiction, shockingly, did not come up.)

Although the initial shock of my daring costumes blew over, I felt as though many parents developed a rather uncalled-for prejudice against me. I was automatically labelled a 'wild child' and had to work extra hard to have friends be allowed to stay over. (My mother interjects here to say that she did not know this.) When friends arrived, they were armed with rules from their mothers. R-rated movies were off-limits, there was an early bedtime and no, we could not go see the movie *Dick*.

---

4   If you live under Ayers Rock and don't know what Capri Suns are, they are 'juice' drinks packaged in floppy silver pouches, and somehow contain more sugar than high fructose corn syrup. They are also freaking impossible to pierce with the straws that come with them, until you figure out how to turn them upside down and use the bottom.

Of course, my reputation didn't get any better after I was caught giving a little sex position lesson during my fifth-grade field trip. My grandmother, Gladys, had bought me a t-shirt on our trip to Sweden that had drawings of various moose doing it missionary, doggy style and 69-ing with the caption, 'It's natural in Sweden'. (Leave it to the Swedes to make this shirt in youth sizes.) Poor Gladys had no idea about the erotic moose Kama Sutra going on all over my chest; she just thought they were hugging.

I admit that when I put three of my Beanie Babies on top of each other to explain what a ménage à trois was to my girlfriends at my birthday party, I may have been crossing the line. The only thing that salvaged my 'paediacocious'[5] reputation was (spoiler alert) that I did not end up having a teen pregnancy and got a college degree.

---

5   Yes, 'paediacociousness' is a new word invented by me that means 'child sexual precociousness'.

LESSONS LEARNT
IN SCHOOL

You're probably wondering how I ended up at a school that didn't kick me out for being a Playboy bunny for Halloween. Finding the right learning environment for us was quite the mission for Donna. She arranged meetings with the local private schools and public schools, and even entertained the idea of boarding school. When an administrator at Martha Manson Academy assured my mom that our learning experience would be just like her own in the 1950s, she said HELL NO. Donna didn't want some psycho lady on a power trip reprimanding her children for being free thinkers.

And that's exactly what I was: a free thinker. Kind of. Let's just say I came out of my mom's belly with two goals: to do anything necessary to solidify a cool-kid reputation and to achieve ultimate stardom. Being the perfect student was definitely not on my agenda.

Don't:
Succumb
to peer
pressure.

As her search for the perfect school continued, Donna sent us to camp at Jordan Glen. JG is an alternative school and summer camp nestled in the small town of Archer, Florida. Summer camp is a really big deal in America. Where else would kids learn to make daisy chains, get hair wraps and partake in archery? And this particularly amazing camp housed hippies, screaming children, pre-teen counsellors (who practised kissing with each other), peacocks, ducks, chickens, cats, dogs and, of course, a pig and a sheep.

It was during my three weeks at JG summer camp that I decided that I needed to return to this magical land, every day, forever. I told Donna that it was the absolute best place in the world for me. Agreeing, she told me to call Jeff, the owner/principal/teacher/sports director, and tell him that I wanted to go to Jordan Glen School. My little five-year-old fingers picked up the phone and dialled 411. (Three things I have been able to do since birth: call 411, operate a microwave and speak at inappropriate times.) I asked for Jeff and informed him that I would like to come to kindergarten that fall, and he accepted me as a full-time student.

Time to start planning my first-day-of-school attire. Back then I was keen on wearing adult-sized t-shirts, cinched at the waist with a fabulous wide black elastic belt. Choosing an outfit would be a no-brainer!

Day one at my new, magical hippie sanctuary was a bit rocky. Working hard to be the cool kid, I more or less immediately collapsed under the pressure of my peers and vandalised the playhouse wall. It took me about six seconds to draw a heart on it with Crayola marker. It took me about an hour to scrub it off. (What kind of first-grade teacher wants to censor love, anyway?)

The next week, a cute blonde girl named Emma talked me into taking the class hamster, Nipsy (short for Sir Nips-a-Lot), on an adventure up to the reading loft. Needing both hands to climb the ladder, I shoved the rodent into my spandex pants and giggled as his nails scraped at my thighs. (I was also really into wearing purple spandex at that time. The fact that this particular pair had stirrups probably saved Nipsy's life.) Apparently, taking the hamster on this journey was *not* okay because our teacher, Debbie, got pretty upset when she saw me playing with him danger-ously close to the railing. I guess she had problems with him hanging a dozen feet above the classroom floor.[1]

As the year progressed, I started to seriously work on my public perception among my peers. How did I impress the wealthy kids who talked about their two-storey homes? I pretended I lived in a wind-up music box–style castle just like the one on the TV show, *Eureeka's Castle*. And how did I outdo all the boys at school? I ate dead worms that had baked in the sun on the sidewalk, while I pranced around in one of my many sequined costumes. (It became an inter-nal battle getting dressed in the morning: mini flamenco dancer costume, or the gold gown from *Beauty and the Beast*?) On top of those efforts, I spent countless hours

---

1   I feel like I shouldn't mention the fate of poor Nipsy, but since this is a tell-all: Emma, that same cute little blonde girl, stepped on him about a month later. RIP, brave little hammy.

watching an array of movies to tell all of my friends about at school: *Double, Double, Toil and Trouble, Don't Tell Mom the Babysitter's Dead, Clueless* and *Jawbreaker*[2].

After Christmas break, school started to get more frustrating. Because, instead of achieving world domination by getting my classmates to think I was cool, I ended up mostly just getting into trouble and being a witness to an unfortunate hamster's horrible death. My plans to make friends by doing what the other kids did were not working and made me a 'follower'. I decided to focus all of my efforts on getting attention by becoming a leader.

Do:
Dabble in
the occult.

It took a few years, but I got my groove back and started dominating elementary school after my best friend, Cherish, and I went to see *The Craft* in the fourth grade. Yes, that movie scared the shit out of us, but we were also completely infatuated. Since Donna had a ouija board, crystals and lots of flowy skirts, we had everything we needed to play '*The Craft* game' after school. (Nothing like a little 'light as a feather, stiff as a board' chanting before homework time.) Turned out, this was our ticket to being cool.

---

2   The image of Marilyn Manson and Rose McGowan having sex in *Jawbreaker* is forever burned into my brain. I will give anyone $100 to make it go away.

Inspired by my new favourite movie, I brought my mom's book on kabbalah to school to practise Jewish mysticism. With our new and mysterious reputation of being witches (kabbalah, sorcery – tomayto, tomahto – no one knew the difference, including us), we would bring curious fellow classmates into the woods behind the school to prove our powers. The kids would tell one of us a number, and then we would explain that we could read each other's minds by holding one another's temples. The one of us who knew the number would squeeze her jaw so that the 'mind-reader' could feel it with her fingertips and count to whatever number the kid was thinking of. This worked every time. (Well, every time until someone guessed above forty and my kid brain couldn't count that high without being off by about three numbers.) While my math skills declined, my coolness levels were steady. The next bump up in popularity came when my psychic self got a training bra, since this is the only time in life where exposed bra straps actually increase your social capital.

As if all these coolness-enhancers weren't enough, you may recall that I was also a Playboy bunny for Halloween the previous year. I was finally at the peak of popularity with my classmates when I was entering the fifth grade which, at Jordan Glen, was like being a freshman in high school. The fifth through to eighth grades were all in one classroom, and each grade (about eight people) sat at a table. Now surrounded by the older kids, I suddenly needed bigger tricks than bra straps and Jewish mysticism to be cool. I decided that my only course was to be obnoxious and outrageous. This involved antics such as shaving my legs in class, dancing on our teacher's desk at lunchtime and, of course, showing off my brand-new (three kilo) Nokia mobile phone.

A Donnalandish Thought on Education:
Sending your daughter to hippie private school: $40,000.
Buying her fishnet stockings in the third grade: $5. Being
able to pick your battles: Priceless.

Do:
Bring fast
times to
Jordan Glen

In seventh grade, my new best friend, Lauren (who replaced
Cherish after she transferred to public school), and I
started obsessing over the movie *Fast Times at Ridgemont
High*. We would fantasise about Ron Johnson sending us
flowers at school, and searched everywhere for a red bikini
that was worthy of Phoebe Cates. The free-swim period at
school was our time to practise the slow-motion walk out of
the pool. (The keys were the hair swing and the eye contact
with the naive blink at the end.)

One day I was feeling particularly daring and decided
to pull a Spicoli by ordering a pizza to be delivered to me at
school. Since our classroom was usually pretty chaotic, our
teacher, Jeff, didn't seem to notice when I crawled under
the table and made a call to Domino's. (I bet Donna is seriously questioning the decision to give her ten-year-old a
credit card and cell phone right about now.) As I ordered
and watched the clock, I started to realise that the pizza was
not going to make it in time for lunch. Suddenly my plan

had a hole in it, and panic was setting in, fast. How was I going to intercept the pie before one of the teachers noticed that I was supposed to be in class? More importantly, I was starving/desperately needed to impress my friends!

Ultimately helpless, I sat through a lunchless lunch hour and then sweated anxiously through science class while watching the door for my imminent embarrassment. As expected, Jeff called me out of class to 'reprimand' me for ordering a pizza at school and causing a disruption. My class snickered as I did the walk of shame out the door. He handed me an empty pizza box and informed me that, as a punishment, he gave all of the teachers a slice. Unable to control my rage (not to mention the fact that I am hypo-glycaemic and become a psycho if I don't eat), I started crying and accused him of stealing, since I had paid for it! (Well, my mom's Visa card had paid for it, but Jeff didn't need to know that.) He let me make an ass of myself for a solid two minutes before he smiled and opened the oven in the school kitchen, showing me the whole pizza. Once I calmed down, we both had a slice and laughed. And yes, it was a *very* cool move.

Don't:
Stick a
tampon in a
dry vagina.

The next step in my quest for coolness was getting my period. Unfortunately, it just wasn't happening. Don't get me wrong, I was really *trying* to shed the lining of my uterus and all, but nope. It wasn't going anywhere. Here's how it all went down.

The second time I lost my virginity was under the stars on a beautiful Florida beach. It was spring break (such a stereotype, I know), the air was warm, the ocean was calm and the moon was bright. He was my first real boyfriend and I just knew that I wanted to make sweet love to him with my eyes closed. Although there were no scented candles, and Boyz II Men was not the soundtrack, the ocean serenaded and guided our bodies on a one-minute journey to an awkward disappointment that I will never forget.

The *first* time I lost my virginity was even less romantic. It all began in the fifth grade. It was my second week of sex education, and we were learning about menstruation. Being a child who could recite *Are You There God? It's Me, Margaret* verbatim, I was thoroughly unimpressed by the teacher's meagre attempt at a lecture. She was droning on about a wall that lined the uterus, and how it exited the body when it was not needed to support a fertilised egg. What I was expecting was for her to tell me that a beautiful, bountiful crimson river would be flowing out of me on a Kotex raft and, at that moment, the world would know that Summer Land was now an enchanted vessel fit for all things womanly.

It was during this class that my teacher mentioned (after much pestering from me) that we could practise using a tampon before our 'gift' officially arrived. Luckily, Donna had recently bought me a pack of tampons 'just in case' I got my period. Later, as I perched on the toilet, chugging a gallon of Yoo-hoo, I could barely contain my excitement. (I don't know why I thought liquids would help, but for some reason I thought I needed a full bladder to menstruate. I guess I wasn't really paying attention in class.) I began the insertion process, to no avail. After numerous failed attempts, hitting what felt like a wall when I tried to push them in, I worked my way through three-quarters of my box of tampons.

Eventually, I found myself in the living room doing lunges on the piano bench while Brett watched *Ren & Stimpy* and Donna did our homework. With my dwindling box of tampons beside me and one leg up on the glossy mahogany bench (just as the illustration in the directions showed), I pushed the second-to-last tampon into my vagina hole. This resulted in one of the most horrific pains I had ever felt. With a quick pull, I ripped that little mouse-tail out of me, moving even quicker than the time I double-palmed our barbecue grill. That's when I saw it. Blood. There was *blood* on the very tip of the tampon! It had happened!!!

Brett yelled out in horror, 'You're so disgusting, Summer!' when he finally noticed what I was doing. But I didn't care.

I screamed, 'DONNA! I GOT IT! I GOT IT! I have my period! I'm gonna need more tampons.'

Donna looked a bit sceptical as she eyed the piece of cotton dangling in front of her. I tried to solidify my case by telling her about the horrific pain I was in, and that I had terrible cramps. Donna put down my vocabulary worksheet and walked over to really examine the blood. This was when the walls of my new exciting womanly world came crashing down just as quickly as they had risen.

Donna pulled me into her lap and gently let me know that the cramps were not menstrual, nor did they have anything to do with my 'gift'. Instead, they were a direct result of shoving a box-worth of tampons into my vagina all day and breaking my hymen.

I was crushed. I knew exactly what a hymen was (having read and carried around *My Body, My Self for Girls* like it was the Bible or the Torah or the Scientology Space

Book for months), so her words hit like a truck. I had stolen my own moment. The moment that was supposed to be reluctantly given away after prom. It would no longer be on the night when I put on that beautiful, sparkly polyester gown and took a picture with my handsome date in front of a stack of blocks that read '2 0 0 5'. I wouldn't be able to think back on that night of forced, awkward intimacy as that momentous 'first time'. Instead, I popped my own cherry with a tiny cotton penis.

A Donnalandish Thought on Pre-marital Sex:

Sex is too good to stay a virgin for too long, but not so great that you need to be in a hurry. I tried to explain this to Summer, but she was in a hurry anyway.

Do: Embrace your unplanned pregnancy.

It seemed like as soon as I broke my hymen, I was faced with thoughts of an unplanned, but wanted, pregnancy. You see, I could not wait to take sex education. Caring for a fake baby for a week was something I really wanted to do. I even got started early in the third and fourth grades by babysitting those school-imposed burdens for older boys who had no intention of doing it themselves. The first year that I babysat, the doll was a two-kilo bag of flour. The second year, the doll was a two-kilo bag of flour wrapped in pink terry cloth with enough fabric at one end to be stuffed and tied into a head. I recall that on one, in particular, someone had drawn a face with a black pen. The poor sack of flour looked terrifying.

The miracle of childbirth has seemingly been on my mind since I took my first breath. Not only was I baffled (and impressed) by my own arrival, but I also started analysing Donna's parenting methods at a very young age. With every game of house I played, I became more and more intrigued by the idea of being a mom. Not the conception or birth part, but the glamorous stroller-pushing, book-reading 'I'm a mom!' part. I imagined the cute bedroom I would give my baby and the clothes I would wrap around its little body. As a self-confessed Spenderella, I was well seasoned in wasting massive amounts of money on things that I (and my future child) didn't need. So I pictured myself bedazzling the crap out of my baby in every way possible. Of course, I was still a responsible make-believe parent, factoring in costs for health insurance, booster shots, yearly check-ups, summer camp, diapers and waiting lists for private schools.

They say that the moment a woman is pregnant she becomes a mother, and the moment a man holds his baby he becomes a father. This is also true for doll-raising. I like to think I got 'pregnant' in sex education class. It seemed like I was constantly on the edge of my seat waiting for the announcement, pressing so hard on my desk that it was slicing a crease into my stomach. Finally, the day came, towards the end of the year. Like all students before me, I would be faced with one of life's greatest challenges: parenting.

I had been preparing for months. Knowing what was best for baby, I had cut Coca-Cola and other caffeinated beverages from my diet. And since I was ten (and not yet into binge drinking), I wasn't too upset when I gave up my pretend glass of red wine with dinner every night (although I was slightly worried about missing out on the precious antioxidants). Feeling clear-minded and ready to devote my life to my baby, I waited patiently as the sex education teacher, Marie, told us the terms of our challenge.

We were to take care of a doll for one week. And, unless the baby was 'napping', we had to hold and care for them as if they were real. This year, the school had invested in actual dolls to replace the previously used (and decidedly un-lifelike) sacks of flour. Unfortunately, they weren't the kind of dolls that cried or urinated (that would have been beyond amazing). Instead, we really just had to carry them around with us wherever we went.

When Marie lined up nine dolls, I knew that the third from the left was the one. He looked like my own flesh and plastic. His name would be Taylor and he was beautiful (just like his mommy). I picked Taylor up and cradled him in my arms. My other classmates weren't ready for their 'babies', but I had brought my baby bag, filled with new baby clothes. (Thank you, American Girl, for making the modern-day dolls so that Taylor didn't look like an eighteenth-century plantation princess from the South.) I dressed him in overalls and a tie-dyed shirt. (God, I love the 90s.) I was a bit disappointed that American Girl wasn't partnered with Tommy Hilfiger; if those overalls had had the TH logo on the straps, Taylor would have been even cuter.

I was a bit nervous when I put Taylor down to sleep that first evening. Even though I had completely transformed my room into a nursery, I think it's natural to worry that they won't sleep through the first night. I found myself just staring at Taylor's beautiful rubber skin and marble-like eyes (which may have actually been marbles). The next day, I decided that it would be great to get some support from the other new moms. I had Donna pick up some fruit and vegie trays from the grocery store, and we organised a baby play-date. All of my classmates came with their little ones in tow, and we spent the day exchanging stories about our newborns. We were all so thankful to have dodged the stretch marks and haemorrhoids that usually accompany baby-having!

It was amazing how quickly a week went by. But what was even more amazing was my newfound appreciation of a mother's love. The more time I spent with Taylor, the more I knew that I was simply not going to be able to give him back on Friday. His constant grin fuelled my affection and my desire to provide for him, forever and always. The night before I had to return Taylor to Marie I found myself pacing in my room, only stopping to peer into Taylor's crib. The hours flew by and my eyes grew tired from watching him. I must have fallen asleep, because I woke up fully clothed and on top of my covers. I quickly brushed my teeth and cradled Taylor in my arms the entire ride to school. It was all happening too fast! I just wanted to freeze time so that I wouldn't have to lose my doll-child.

At lunch, I finally broke down. Unable to stand the idea of not caring for T-Man anymore, I called my mom and told her that I couldn't do it. I couldn't go to sex education and have them take my baby. I had made a promise to Taylor that I would ALWAYS be there for him, and I wasn't about to give up. I was fully prepared to go into a custody battle with the school, but any lawyers I knew were too busy to get involved with doll cases (especially for the amount that a ten-year-old could afford to pay them). So, instead, Donna came through with a wonderful solution. We ended up buying a replacement doll for the school! I was so relieved. I was also positive that I would never be able to foster anything else due to my irreparable attachment issues.

I continued to take care of Taylor for another week or so. But then I got a new bike (with pegs!) and soon forgot about him. He hangs out in the attic now. I'm pretty sure he hooked up with Baby Uh-Oh, but maybe that's just gossip from my Cabbage Patch doll.

A Donnalandish Thought on Parenting:

Brett used to always go to skateboard camp in the summer with his best friend, Stephen. One year, his friend's mom said that Stephen couldn't go if he didn't make good grades at school. Horrified, Brett asked me if I would ever do that to him. I said no way, because if you're not good at academics you're going to need a back-up plan.

LESSONS LEARNT ABOUT YOUNG LOVE

Being a single mom was hard. What was harder was being the only single sixth-grade girl at school.

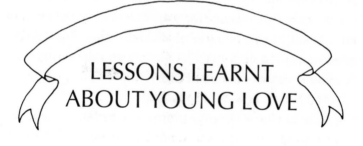

Do:
Hold hands
with boys.

I remember my first boyfriend like I remember my own name. I actually still know his home address and phone number by heart, even though I never went to his house or actually called him on the phone. Anyway, this was a very serious relationship, as sixth-grade commitments go. When you're eleven and dating one of the coolest boys in your grade (even though I went to a tiny hippie private school in rural Florida with only nine people in the entire grade), it's pretty easy to mistake forced, awkward hand-holding as love. Mostly, I was blinded by male attention. But it didn't take me long to discover that our entire relationship had been nothing more than ONE. BIG. LIE.

And here is how it all happened.

I was having a sleepover with some eighth-grade girls, and we were in the middle of an intense game of Truth or Dare. My turn came up and I was asked the inevitable, 'Summer, who do you have a crush on?' My mind went blank. I did not really have feelings for anything besides My Little Ponies and my *Rocky Horror Picture Show* VHS tape, much less an actual person. But I knew that I had to think of a name to say because I desperately wanted their attention and still needed to be cool. I mean, Holly and Marissa already had their periods and above average–sized boobs! Time for a quick mental inventory of the four males in my grade.

One was the new kid, who would normally be a safe bet, but he was a little too cocky for my liking. Another had a twin (bonus), but seemed too nerdy. The third was a massive, beastly man-child who spent most of his time being kicked out of different schools and getting sent to the principal's office. Even at age eleven, I knew that I needed more stability than that from a life partner. That left me with the fourth: a nice boy who seemed a little shy, but had a good sense of humour and was wickedly smart. So I said his name to the girls so we could move on. Unfortunately for me, this opened the floodgates for Holly and Marissa to join forces with Lauren to play matchmaker. These girls were a cupid trifecta.

As the natural progression of middle-school relation-ships go, my friend first told his friend that I liked him. Then his friend told my friend that he liked me too. Then I told my friend to tell his friend to tell him that I really, really liked him. Then he told his friend who told my friend who told me that he wanted me to be his main squeeze.

Suddenly, there we were: boyfriend and girlfriend. Everything was so effortless in the beginning. I would tell my friend to tell his friend that he looked really cute one day. And then he would tell his friend to tell my friend that he thought I looked really hot. Then his friends would conspire with my friends and coerce us into sweaty hand-holding during lunch. We had been dating pretty seriously at school for a month or so when my phone rang one after-noon. It was him. He asked me out on a proper date. (Funny how the commitment came before our first date.) We were going to see a movie, and his mom was going to drive us.

After spending hours obsessing over what to wear, I settled on a skort and a simple white baby-t (with the blue Gap logo placed strategically over my breast buds). The outfit was completed with a matching blue scrunchie on my wrist, platform jelly shoes and socks neatly folded at the ankles. I do not remember the ride to the theatre, but I do remember the adrenaline rush that followed, due to sitting next to a boy in a dark room for the first time ever. We went to see Gwyneth Paltrow in *Sliding Doors*. I have NO IDEA who chose that one, but it was great background noise as our elbows clinked and our shoulders grazed during our awkward leans. Finally, a nervous pinkie poked my palm and glided itself into a legitimate hand-hold. One hour and forty-five minutes later, I was in love.

Two weeks after that, it was Valentine's Day. Seeing as we never spoke to each other, and our quality time con-sisted of going to the movies in silence, I was not sure what to get him. I also was not sure what he was going to get me. So I decided to play it safe and get him a giant tin of jelly beans. Who doesn't love a flavoured candy in the shape of a high-protein plant seed? I could only hope for something equally as thoughtful/calorie-laden from him. And he certainly delivered.

Two incredible things happened in 1997. One, *Titanic* was released, and two, on that very Valentine's Day, I received my first box of chocolates from a boy. But not just *any* box of chocolates: it was a beautiful, oversized, velvet, heart-shaped container, filled with succulent caramel truffles. There was no way I could open it. I felt silly not indulging in the candies with my friends, but I knew I would soon have to shrink-wrap and mummify the gift to be kept in its original state as a relic, and place it in my middle-school boyfriend shrine. Oh, and he also gave me a rose. Swoon! At that moment, I knew what the 'he loves me, he loves me not' flower was saying. No matter what, 'he definitely loves me.'

Or not?

February faded and spring had officially arrived in Florida. The only thing not blossoming was our love. One of his friends told one of my friends that he had never even liked me in the first place, and that he had only gone out with me as a dare. (Cue: black mascara cascading down my cheeks and emotional devastation. Stay tuned for: Summer shows first warning signs of being a complete psychopath when it comes to dating.) I was LIVID! First of all, I didn't even really like him in the first place either! I only said that I did to seem cool to the older girls. Secondly, I was taller than he was! Thirdly, I gave him jelly beans! OMFGWTF???

There was only one thing that could possibly make me feel better and less vulnerable: public humiliation of my now ex-boyfriend. I came up with a scheme that would involve some careful execution and smooth-talking. It all began with a visit to our schoolbus driver, Ona. Woefully, I explained how I had been brutally wronged by my one and only, and needed to smash his heart the way he had smashed mine. That's right, I talked Ona into running over the box of chocolates a few times with our school bus. Once I was satisfied with the tyre prints branded into the velvet, I strolled up to my ex while he was hanging out with all of his friends at lunch. I proceeded to hurl the squashed box at his chest and announce, 'I don't need your box of chocolates, and they mean nothing to me! It's funny – I was actually dared to go out with you, too. I guess we both win.' I glared for a moment, then whipped my hair and stormed away a new woman.

Of course, old flames die hard. But if you truly love something, then you must let it go. And I did. I loved myself, and then I let myself go completely apeshit. (The ex and I eventually made up and became friends, as all lovers should.)

By the way, I highly suggest becoming friends with at least one bus driver – just in case you need him to run over something or someone for you.

Do: Put toe blood in your sibling's mouth.

Thankfully I managed to dodge another heartbreak for the rest of the year. I decided to focus on myself and my passions, such as acting and dance. But I was still in a very unhealthy, some might say abusive, relationship with my brother. The more he rejected me, the more I needed him to like me. One afternoon, Brett's friends Jesse and Skylar were over playing WAR. (In case you don't know, WAR is a game where you dress up in camo and play with the 'artillery' your mom bought you at Walmart.) I wanted to play too, so I started loading up Brett's paintball gun. Before I knew it, I had launched three giant splats of pink against Brett's bedroom wall. Oooops. Brett ran in and saw his wall, which now looked more like a Lisa Frank folder than a boy's room.

He screamed, 'Summer, you better layer up!'

This could only mean one of two things. One, we were going to the snow, or two, he was about to shoot me with his BB gun. Fuck. It was #2. As I sprinted down our hallway and into my room, I managed to fling a sand-weighted tape dispenser directly at Brett's head in an attempt to deter him. I didn't want to stick around to see if I'd made contact, so I quickly barricaded myself in my room.

Brett started shooting under my door. I screamed out for Donna over the sound of the BB pellets zinging into my room, while Jesse and Skylar laughed uncontrollably. Snot and tears streamed down my face as the zings slowed down and Brett's footsteps shuffled down the stairs. Just as I was trying to figure out how to murder him and dispose of his body (I did still have that trunk for summer camp ...) I smelled something amazing. It was Papa John's pizza. Clearly dinner had arrived. I knew that in order for me to get that pizza, I had to face my brother and apologise. I slowly pushed my chair away from in front of my door and headed downstairs. Since Brett seemed pretty distracted by chugging the side cups of butter sauce[1],

---

1   If butter sauce on pizza is wrong, I don't want to be right.

I felt safe to sit down. Afraid to fuel the fire, I told him I'd wash the paint off his wall. Surprisingly, he pushed the pizza towards me.

Just when you think that you really wouldn't care if someone died, they share their pizza with you and it's all over. I was right back to loving him.

When my friends at school would tell me stories about their boyfriends emotionally neglecting them and treating them like crap (like choosing to sit with the boys at lunch or not writing back to a note), I always advised them that they deserved the world and should drop those douche bags like a bad habit. But when they'd tell me that they made up and were back together, I never judged because that's exactly how I always was with my brother.

One time, Brett and his friends enthusiastically called me in to his room to tell me about a new flavour of marshmallows. I grabbed what I thought was a handful of this delightful new creation and shoved them into my mouth. Instead of a burst of sugary goodness, an explosion of sour urine filled my mouth. Yes, the boys had completely soaked the marshmallows with their own pee. Brett laughed hysterically. I cried, internalised my hatred and silently declared war. There was no way I could forgive him after this.

Most of the time, I went with the easy stuff: stealing the remote control, eating the last popsicle, and (my favourite) biting myself, crying, and then blaming my brother. I discovered that teeth marks equalled Brett being scolded because there was undeniable physical evidence. Unfortunately, my acting out only fuelled my brother's wrath. At school, he would steal my shoes and throw them on the roof. During lunch, he would grab my food and shove all of the bologna in his mouth (he only needed the Heimlich manoeuvre once), so that I wouldn't get any. At home, he would blame every single thing he did wrong on me. (By the way, Donna, the Gak on our six-metre ceilings was actually *neither* of us. It was Alek. I swear.)

But then he would do something nice, like let me go with him and his friends to a skateboard park. One day, he spent an hour helping me learn how to drop in on a ramp. I even mastered this trick before one of his best friends did, which clearly made him proud to be my brother.

Years later, a fifteen-year-old Summer was walking into the house when Brett thought it would be funny to hock a loogie on her from the balcony. His saliva bomb missed, but I had to release my anger because my body had not yet figured out how to control the delicate balance of hormones that were trying to take me into womanhood. I found myself running over to his car, hoisting my body onto the hood and stomping on it repeatedly. Double stomp. (Yeah, I know. Rough.) I quickly ran away, only to be tracked down by Donna, who now had to pay the $1000 worth of damage.[2]

Sometimes if you really love someone, you need to get as far away as possible from them. Choosing separate cities for college allowed us to both mature (kind of) and come back home as more nostalgic and caring people. For instance, after I'd graduated from college, Brett, Jesse, Skylar and I were all sitting at a bar when I noticed that my toe was bleeding. It was pretty gross, and blood got all over my finger when I was trying to dress the wound with a straw wrapper. In front of everyone, Brett yelled, 'EWWWWW, period blood!'

Young Summer might have chucked the dummy there, but Newly Matured Summer laughed and tried to run her bloody finger across his moustache while yelling

---

2   This was not the only time I've cost my mom an unnecessary amount of money. See: Summer Land's $2500 cell phone bill of August 2002. Apparently I was roaming. And apparently there are charges for that.

'Dirty Sanchez!'[3] Unfortunately, I was unsuccessful in my attempt. My finger slipped into his mouth and my bloody, jagged nail scraped across his gums.

A wave of fear washed over me. Was he going to kill me? Was this the end? Of course, he was disgusted (rightfully so) and drank a shot of whisky to recover. After clarifying that I didn't have AIDS, we hugged it out. He ended up getting my name tattooed on his wrist as a way to show that no matter how much he hated me, he really did love me. Guess a finger-full of toe blood to the mouth will make you do just about anything.

Don't:
Be a
Lewinsky.

But let's go back to a time where blood wasn't the bodily fluid I was worried about. Although Donna managed to find the perfect elementary/middle school for me, we collectively struggled to find a decent solution for high school. I was initially accepted to the International Baccalaureate program at Eastside High School, but knew that spending copious hours on math and science was definitely not going to make me the coolest of the cool. Instead I ended up choosing Buchholz High School because my bestie from middle school, Lauren, went there, and I really wanted

---

3   If you don't know what a Dirty Sanchez is, you need to Google it. Just don't do it at work.

a spot on their dance team, Aviance. Lauren had been a member for a year. AND she performed on *The Today Show* during the Macy's Thanksgiving Day Parade. At fourteen, that was pretty much the pinnacle of coolness in my book.

Earning a spot on the team the summer before freshman year definitely made my transition from hippie middle school to public school much more enjoyable. I had a group, an identity and an after-school activity. I also had twelve-hour weekend practices. Our coach, Vicki, took her job seriously. Like, super-duper seriously. We had an entire class period dedicated to our dance team, and then three-hour practices after school. We all worked on a point system. If we arrived to practice any later than FIFTEEN MINUTES PRIOR to our practice start time, it was minus five points. If we forgot our water bottles, it was minus five points. If we didn't have both our right and left splits, it was minus ten points. We walked to a whistle and always stood with our hands behind our backs when we were not performing. I have to hand it to Vicki – her drill-sergeant approach made us amazing and extremely punctual dancers.

During the autumn we would perform in the half-time show at football games. As a result of being part of the half-time show, we were required to attend band camp. I'm not exaggerating when I say this: band kids love sex. They are the most sexually charged group I have ever come in contact with, and I've even been on Birthright.[4]

It was there that I met my crush, a trumpet-player named Randy. I kind of judged his instrument choice at first (I had always pictured myself with a bass player, that's all), but Donna told me to be nice to the band kids, since they were the most likely to grow up to be rock stars. I didn't dwell on it too much though, because he was a junior and

---

4 Birthright is an organised trip to Israel for young Jewish people. Way more on that later.

I was a freshman and he was *so* out of my league. There was no chance he'd ever even notice me. I was also so tired from my extreme dance schedule that I couldn't even think about flirting.

Around the six-month mark of nonstop dancing, I started to get a little antsy and began to wonder what else was out there. How come the cheerleaders and football players always looked like they were having so much more fun? They looked like they were straight out of *Varsity Blues*. Aviance dancers looked like the soldiers in *Schindler's List*.

Instead of putting in the extra hours really stretching out my left split, I started hanging out with this popular blonde bombshell named Sarah. The thing about Sarah was that she wasn't monogamous with one social group. She knew a tonne of people, and seemed to have a place in every clique. She also totally made out with boys, so I just had to know her. We bonded through a mutual friend, and thus began an everlasting friendship based on boys, Jell-O shots and sisterly love.

Our first adventure began when a bunch of us piled out of a car and onto the lawn in front of a senior boy's house party. His giant brick home was lit beautifully. I started imagining what it would be like to live there. The sidewalk was so clean that I'd have licked tapioca off it without hesitation. Everything, from the grass to the shrubs to the azaleas, was perfectly manicured. This was totally the kind of house I'd want to go trick-or-treating at.

Sarah rang the doorbell.

I popped in a piece of Big Red gum and crumpled the wrapper into my purse. Just as I was going to use some cinnamony spit to fix my hair, the door swung open. DJ Sammy's 'Heaven' was blasting through the house. We walked in and gave our shy little introductions. It quickly became obvious that someone must have had a fake ID, because there was plenty of beer to go around. I declined the offer of a nice cold Natural Light[5], but did take a seat at the dining room table with some other people. And who also happened to be sitting at that very table but Randy. My trumpet player.

The tension around the table loosened when someone suggested that we play Never Have I Ever. If you don't know how to play, it's pretty self-explanatory. Basically, you sit around in a circle with friends and someone says something that they've never ever done. Whoever HAS done that thing has to take a drink. Of course, the topic is always sex, drugs or embarrassing mishaps. Seeing as I was a fourteen-year-old ninth-grader and hadn't even gone to second base, I actually had a decent amount of nevers. After one girl admitted that she'd had sex in her parents' bed, I decided I needed to pull out the big guns to get these guys to think I was cool. So I pulled out a pair of Dirty Dice.

I wasn't sexually active at the time, and had no real plans for them; I just thought they were funny and wanted to show them off. I had bought them at Spencer's like five years previously. Now, they really got the party going. Before I knew it, we were playing spin the bottle. When the Bud Light bottle landed in the dead centre of me and Sarah, there was really only one logical thing to do: make out. So yeah, that was the first time I ever made out with a girl for attention. And yes, it worked. My free spirit and naivety only made it that much easier for me to become a Marilyn instead of a Jackie. Randy really started to warm up to me.

It's safe to say that I was drunk on male attention, because the next thing I knew, Randy grabbed my hand and guided me to his friend's bedroom. As we made our

---

5   Seeing as I had never consumed alcohol, I wasn't about to waste my first time on a Natural Light.

way there, I took in his tanned, even-toned skin and tousled dark hair and relished the fact that he had chosen *me*. I consulted the game book in my head, considering my play. After some brief thought, I decided to let him get to third base, since I hadn't developed any boobs to touch. But, oh shit, I had my period! (Commence internal 'Fuck fuck fuck, what am I going to do?' deliberation: 'Maybe he won't try … What if he tries to have sex with me? … I don't want to have sex … I just want to make out with this guy and maybe let him feel me up … No … Fuck.')

As my mind was vacillating between fingering and periods, Randy locked the door and we began to make out. In no time, we were awkwardly dry-humping on the bed. I was stressing the whole time, and didn't want him to go down my pants. Thinking back, I don't know why I didn't think it would be acceptable to just say, 'I'm not ready for that' or, at least, 'Hey man, I'm on the rag. Sorry.' But, for some reason, it didn't cross my mind.

When he reached for my zipper, I did what any not-ready-to-lose-her-virginity virgin would do: I flipped on top of him and took control. (Important sidenote: I had never seen a penis in real life at that point. The closest I'd gotten was watching HBO's *Real Sex*, at the age of five, with Brett. Donna caught us in the living room with our eyes glued on the TV as HBO studied the many different shapes and sizes of penises from around the world. Naturally, Donna didn't want us to think that there was anything wrong with the human body, so she sat down with us to discuss genitalia.) As I undid Randy's jeans and slid his boxer shorts down, I remember being a little grossed out. A fleshy member, surrounded by coarse black pubic hair, flopped out.

I had only recently gotten hair down there and had about twenty-five pubes (yes, I counted). But this boy's bush would make even Ron Jeremy look like he manscaped. Despite this, I proceeded to give what was probably one of the least confident blow jobs in history, for the next five minutes.

I really don't know how I knew what to do, but things seemed to be going smoothly when, all of the sudden, he secreted something. In my mouth. Without warning. For a second, I thought it was pee. My mind raced until, finally, a light bulb went off: it was sperm! Gross! I was so revolted that I spit it into my lap. And it immediately hardened onto my pants like Krazy Glue. In a blur of 'oh-my-goodness-I-just-gave-a-blow-job', Randy stood and kissed me on the cheek. I quickly scampered out of the room to go brag to all of my girlfriends about giving head. It didn't occur to me that sharing these shenanigans might be a bad idea.

As the party died down and couples trickled off to different bedrooms, Sarah and I headed back to a friend's house. Since I wasn't at my own place, I couldn't change clothes. (I don't think my friend's jeans fit. That, or I was, in some way, proud of my dirty denim.) So, I went to school the next day in the only outfit I had: a wrinkly top and a pair of sperminated jeans. Of course, I was oblivious and thought it was hysterical that I had sperm on my pants.

By about lunchtime, it was apparent that I had actually been doing the walk of shame for four class periods. It suddenly dawned on me that the whispers weren't nice, and that not everyone was impressed. I was devastated. To me, giving head to an older guy was going to be the coolest thing since pants with pockets. I mean, there was hard evidence that I had successfully blown a guy!

My closest friends knew the truth: that I wasn't a slut and really did like Randy. But everyone else wasn't so kind. Turned out Randy didn't like the attention either, especially since he was running for school president. He completely blew me off. (That wasn't exactly the favour I wanted in return.)

I didn't get it. It seemed like hooking up with guys was the 'cool' thing to do. A month later, I got a steady boyfriend named Ryan and tightened up my loose reputation as best I could. It wasn't until the spring, when it was time for the seniors to graduate and move on to college, that my 'indiscretion' came back to life. I got out of Donna's car and casually strolled to my locker, only to be greeted by a friend with a school newspaper. There it was, on The Senior Will[6] page, my claim to freshman fame:

> To Summer, I leave you Monica Lewinsky's phone number. She knows a great drycleaner to get that spot out of your jeans.

Do:
Have friends in high places.

I know that there is no such thing as bad publicity, but being called out for having sperm on my pants at school was reason enough for me to get out of town for a while. A couple of months after the incident, I decided to go on vacation with one of my other besties, Laura, and her family.

---

6   This is a section in the student newspaper where seniors leave things to lower-classmen, like parking spots, calculators and hall passes. Why they couldn't have left me a prime locker spot is beyond me ...

Laura and I met while on a cruise of the Baltic when we were ten. My grandmother, Gladys, always felt that travel was the best form of education, and loved taking Brett and me on exotic trips. Luckily for me, Laura's parents were also avid travellers. Laura and I bonded in Denmark when we were too small to ride the rental bikes on an outing.

She lived in upstate New York, where her dad had one of those jobs where you have no idea what he does, but you know that he never goes to an office and is extremely well-off. I think he used to work in banking, but when I knew him, he mostly played with his Porches and Apple gadgets. They were such a fun family to visit. (Especially because they had houses in New York[7], Vermont and Martha's Vineyard.) And this time, her family invited me to the Bahamas!

We spent day one relaxing by the Atlantis Resort pool, on Paradise Island. Her parents were out and about while the two of us had some much needed 'we time'. After scarfing down $16 burgers and lubing ourselves up with Banana Boat SPF-4 tanning oil (I'd promised Donna I would wear sunscreen), we started playing coy with the cute boys on the other side of the pool. Life was good.

---

7   One of the first times I went to visit Laura in New York, I had my first kiss. Since it was 2001 and *Save the Last Dance* was really popular, we weren't listening to much other than K-Ci & JoJo and, of course, watching that movie religiously. One night, two of Laura's guy friends came over and we went down to her basement to sneak some of her parents' alcohol and listen to 'Crazy' and 'All My Life' (on repeat). (There might have also been a little 3LW 'No More' playing as well.) I didn't drink at this point, but I did have some hormones that I couldn't control! It wasn't long before we had an awkward middle-school dance session going on between the four of us. I was slow dancing (hands on shoulders) with Cam, a smooth-talking black guy with a New York accent. Since all of my friends had been slowly losing their first-kiss virginities, I kept fantasising that Cam would be my first. When he moved his hand off my waist to pop a piece of gum in his mouth, I knew my first kiss could be only moments away. Boy, was I right. Within seconds, that sweet cinnamon taste was engulfing my mouth. His supple lips were so soft, and felt literally all-consuming. The Julia Stiles inside of me was twirling as I tried to remain calm and figure out how to kiss him back. It was a pretty epic first kiss, as those things go.

Soon enough, both of us were getting lost in Usher's *8701* album on our new Discmans and relating (a little too closely) to 'U Got It Bad'. The only time I removed my headphones was when a sweet Bahamian waitress came to take our drink order. Our parched voices requested two Bahama Mamas, and we rolled over to brown our backs. About ten minutes later, the waitress returned with our drinks. After taking two massive gulps, we immediately looked at each other in astonishment.

THEY WERE ALCOHOLIC!

The liquor traced through my blood and, feeling like I had just done a massive sneeze, I enjoyed the euphoric head rush. I was shocked that someone was actually *serving* me an alcoholic beverage! We broke into a hysterical fit of giggles, finished our cocktails and quickly ordered another round (courtesy of her parents' tab). I had moved on to a Mudslide when her mom, Nancy, walked up to say hi and check on us. She approached calmly, but we were obviously failing to 'play it cool' as we gave her overexcited greetings. Making eye contact was slightly uncomfortable.

She picked up Laura's drink to take a sip. Naturally, we decided that this would be a good time to start lying. The two of us explained that we had NO IDEA that there was alcohol in our refreshments and just thought we were light-headed from the heat. This was when I realised that I was a horrible liar (especially while buzzed) and that Laura should probably smooth this one over. (Along with every future lie we would tell her mom/dad/other adults in authority.)

At dinner that night we got a small, figurative slap on the wrist, but were ultimately in the clear. We ate our lobsters in peace while trying to be as apologetic and angel-like as possible ... that was, until we spotted the same cute boys we had seen earlier at the pool. Laura and I silently agreed we suddenly needed to go to the bathroom together and excused ourselves.

Immediately after passing the concierge, we detoured straight to our crushes and used a well-devised icebreaker: we asked them if they would take our picture. It was the perfect opening line. Not only did it start a 'where-are-you-from' conversation, but it also allowed us to pose and show off our Body by Victoria padded bras, along with our new clothes from Rave.[8] When they offered us compliments and Bacardi Limons, we knew these boys were everything two mischievous girls could wish for. The plan was for us to meet up at 9 p.m. in the lobby.

After regaining her parents' trust, Laura and I finagled our way to a night out on our own. Eagerly, we waited for the elevator while checking each other's make-up and clothes. Agreeing on each other's hotness level (I was wearing a baby-blue terry cloth tube top … enough said), we confidently approached our new dates, and thus began my very first drunken adventure. The four of us snuck onto the roof of the resort and ended up climbing a rickety ladder up to one of the towers. As we continued drinking, my face went numb and my eyes started playing tricks on me. Any movements felt heavy, yet light. Fast, but slow. The complete sensory experience of opposition was blowing my mind. I had absolutely no concept of time, but was acutely aware of the humour I was finding in almost everything. I remember thinking that the sounds of words were funny, and I was constantly cackling hysterically. Eventually, someone had the brilliant idea to go swimming. So, we carefully made our way back down the dilapidated ladder and towards the pool. (Probably not the best idea when completely legless from

---

8   These were the kind of clothes that were most likely flammable and definitely not 'made locally and sustainably'.

drinking.) With no other options, we stripped down to our underwear and cannonballed our way into the water. Splish. Splash. Giggle. Spin. Touch. Feel. Flashlight. Security.

Apparently, what had felt like one hour of fun had actually been five. It was 2 a.m. And, as Laura and I were informed that we were both Code Adams (missing persons), we began to sober up and lose our sense of invincibility. I reached for my top, but only found one of the boys' button-ups. Holding our heads down in shame, we walked to the resort's security desk, where Laura's parents were waiting. I'm pretty sure they could smell our flammable breath from ten feet away. I felt cold, wet, drunk and embarrassed, and I also really missed my tube top.

As I look back, I realise that night was a series of firsts (but not lasts) for me. It was the first time I got drunk, the first time I lied about where I was going, the first time I was a missing person (unless you count that one time at Disney World when I was four), and the first of many times Laura and I would disappoint her parents. But it was also the first of myriad ridiculously fun, alcohol-infused nights.

Don't:
Tell your boyfriend you cheated when you didn't.

And then I did something even worse than lying to parents. I lied to Ryan. I told him that I had made out with one of those cute boys. WHY? Why on earth would I do such a thing? Seriously, self: WTF?

When I got back from our trip, I was hanging out with Ryan and his friend Matt. We were all drinking beer, which marked my second alcoholic experience. I don't know if it was the second beer or my own insecurities, but I felt the need to make Ryan jealous. So I said that I had kissed someone in the Bahamas. I could see the hurt wash across his face.

I loved Ryan. And I knew he loved me. As far as high-school relationships went, we were totally each other's first loves. Now, I knew that I couldn't very well take it back. Nope, instead I began to grovel and apologise for hours on end. Eventually he forgave me and we tried to move on the best we could. Too bad his family had a trip planned for us the next month. To the exact same resort.

I was back where it all started.

'Is this where it happened?'

'No, here.'

We were staring at one of the thousand lawn chairs around the pool. I couldn't believe how easily I kept lying. 'We were swimming and then decided to get some air over there. He sat me down and kissed me. I swear I didn't mean to kiss him back, but I was drunk.'

Silence.

'I'm sorry, I really am.'

And I really was. Not for the make-believe cheating part, but the lying part. This was how I learned just how annoying and inconvenient lying is. It's also incredibly irritating and taxing when you lie about something you did *wrong*. Then you're constantly trying to get forgiveness and just make it all go away. It took months for us to move past my 'indiscretion'.

*Don't:
Get caught.*

As if I wasn't already thinking about Ryan 24/7. Now, around eight months in, Donna was constantly asking me about our relationship. She had met Ryan on numerous occasions, but still didn't really *know* him. He was incredibly shy and quiet and I wasn't in a huge 'emotional sharing' phase with my mom at the time. I had a boyfriend, therefore Donna got put on the backburner. But nearly every day after school, she would hit me with the mandatory one million questions: What do his parents do? How old is he, again? Does he drive? What's his tennis ranking? Is he Jewish? You know, the standard stuff. But then, after months of avoiding this topic, she asked the one that haunted me in my sleep:

'Do you need birth control?'

'Mom! NO WAY! I do not need birth control.' (I'd gotten it the month before when I went to visit my friend in Wilmington. I'd gulped a fiery mouthful of moonshine and grabbed a month's worth of Ortho Tri-Cyclin out of her bathroom.)

'But seriously, Mom, I am not doing it. I swear.'

I was totally doing it. In the span of six months I had gone from virginal girl who accidentally gave head to a trumpet player to a full-blown sexually active teenager who Dr Phil would totally lecture. Even though I felt like shouting from a mountain top to my best friends, I didn't feel like sharing this eventful news with my mom. Up to that point I had always been open and honest, but something happened in high school where I became a hormonal, secretive, bitchy teenager. Anyway, at the time I had a lot on my mind, like getting my learner's permit. Little did I know this permit was about to open more than the driver's door to my new car.

And, two weeks later ...

'Please read the last two lines.'

'A D F G K L M ... 3 F W K Q V B.'

'Okay. Take a seat over there and look into the lens. No. You can't smile. [*Click.*] Your card will be ready in about five minutes.'

FIVE whole minutes!? I sat in the plastic chair with absolutely no patience. My foot rattled violently while I chewed off all of my fingernails. I glanced into my compact mirror to see if any flakes of my Hard Candy Red Shimmer nail polish had lodged in my teeth. I didn't want my picture to look like I had a bloody case of gingivitis. Continuing to bite, I ripped back too much skin and shuddered as I had to suck the blood from my pinkie. (These are the things I do when I'm anxious.) I mean, I was about to receive my learner's permit! Not quite as amazing as a full-on driver's licence, but it was still exciting.

My mind raced at the thought of what my picture would look like. Never had I so carefully picked out my outfit: a navy blue Tommy Hilfiger shirt and a khaki skort. (Apparently, they do *not* take a full-body shot for your permit picture.) Suddenly, I felt the need to make sure I hadn't missed anything during my prep that morning. Hair pulled back and sprayed with Rain hairspray (check). Two symmetrical strands dangling in the front to frame my eyes (check; why this hairstyle was ever popular, I will never know). And the final touch: the Return to Tiffany's necklace I received for my bat mitzvah (check). It seemed like I had taken care of everything, so now I just had to wait to make sure my cuteness fully came through in the final picture.

I eventually found distraction in staring at a woman with a mullet. While I was imagining what it would be like to braid the long part, I heard my name called over the intercom.

'Summer Land.'

I don't want to brag or anything but, as pictures of fifteen-year-olds go, I looked phenomenal. No acne (thanks, Maybelline), flawless hair and the finest jewellery a high-schooler could ever wish for (thanks, Roseman family!). I was so excited to have this shiny, awesome card with my picture on it to put in my wallet! It would sit next to my school photo (not quite as flattering), a Rave gift card and Donna's credit card. Not only was I thrilled to be able to operate machinery, but I was also incredibly relieved. The upcoming summer months would be spent on Martha's Vineyard with Laura, and I desperately needed to prove that I could facilitate the transfer from beach to town.

Day one of driving was peaceful, as it mostly consisted of cruising around the neighbourhood. Day two was gradually more stressful, as we ventured onto banked roads and into areas with speed limits in excess of 35 miles per hour. But day three proved to be disastrous. I was driving my mom around in her Hyundai Santa Fe when my brand-new flip phone rang. Like a seasoned driving pro, I pressed pause on my 3LW CD and went to answer.

'Sarah! How are you? ... That's cool ... Yeah. I'm driving at the moment ... What? My mom won't shut up. Hold on— [then, to Donna:] MOM! I am trying to drive. What the fuck!? Gahhhhd! Well, fine! Why don't you just drive then!?'

And that was when I decided to turn in to a gas station so she could do just that. If Donna was going to be such a back-seat driver, then she could take over! I jerked the wheel to the right. Hard. Unfortunately, I was in the middle lane and failed to notice the car to my immediate right. As my hands switched from ten and two to one and eight, our mid-sized SUV slammed itself (okay, I slammed it) into an unsuspecting white pick-up truck. There was the clamour of cars crunching and two generations of women simultaneously screaming 'Fuck!', but all parties involved still managed to pull over into the gas station. An exchange of 'Are you okay' and 'What the fuck were you thinking?' took place until the cops arrived.

A balding officer approached me with a rotund sidekick in tow. Turned out, I'd screwed up the number-one rule of learning how to drive: you're supposed to actually have your licence on you. And mine was in my other purse (the one for going 'out' out, not just out). So we had to call Ryan's mom, Yvonne, to bring it to me from her house.

As Donna sternly reminded me that I was absolutely brain dead and that I should have been drowned at birth, Yvonne pulled up in her white Cadillac Escalade. Standing at about four feet nothing, she hopped down from the driver's seat with my purse. The only thing more awkward than their first meeting was when the police officer asked us to clarify which one was my mother. Donna is brunette. I'm blonde. Yvonne is blonde. Therefore, I must be Yvonne's child. (This proves my point that people simply can't differentiate between blondes.)

Once it was sorted whose womb I came from, we carried on. The rest was pretty standard, as far as car accidents go. There was a lot of standing around, paperwork and 'That could have been so much worse' talk. Finally, I was handed my ticket and got back in the car with my mom. A self-confessed hypochondriac, I started complaining that my shoulder and stomach were really bothering me, and I needed to go to the ER, right away. So, of course, Donna took her battered car and vacuous daughter to the hospital.

Donna and I patiently waited in the comfort of our sticky (with what, I am not sure) plastic emergency-room chairs. From there, we watched a man who was practising Lamaze breathing wipe the sweat from his forehead as he explained to the emotionally vacant receptionist that he thought he had kidney stones. Unamused, she sent him to take a seat next to us. Witnessing the guy's struggle to birth crystallised urine from his urethra, I thought to myself how much I wasn't looking forward to labour. Which led me to my next thought: *I hope I'm not pregnant.* (Even though I was using condoms obsessively, I had an irrational fear of pregnancy.)

The doctor who called us back was young and handsome and probably fresh out of medical school at the University of Florida. I explained that we had just been in a car accident and that my shoulder and stomach really hurt. He decided that I needed a CAT scan, so he had to ask the preliminary questions: Do you smoke or consume alcohol? Do you have any jewellery on? Is there any chance you could be pregnant?

Fifteen-year-old Summer freaked out and murmured, 'No, I don't drink or smoke.' (Lies on the drinking part.) 'Yes, I have a belly-button ring.' (Embarrassing.) And then I paused. I thought back over the past couple of months. Every time a First Response commercial came on, my OCD self would immediately change the channel. I told myself that if I changed it quickly enough, I couldn't be pregnant. Now my mind was reeling: HAD I WATCHED TOO MUCH?

'And yes, I could be pregnant.'

Donna whacked my shoulder with the back of her hand and cried, 'I KNEW IT!'

And that's how my mom found out I was sexually active. In hindsight, a nice heart-to-heart over a bowl of ice-cream may have been a little less detrimental to our relationship, but whatever. I'm special.

After a few tests, it was determined that I had a cyst on my spleen. Who knows why, or if it's still there, but that was all! I have never been so relieved to find out I have a sac of fluid clinging to one of my organs. It was so much better than a foetus. I was told to rest and not engage in contact sports. I was also given a prescription for birth control. To my mother's dismay, the hospital was not in a position to give me a lobotomy.

A Donnalandish Thought on Telling the Truth

Truth will always set you free.

When I was in high school, I used to go up to the top of a mountain with my boyfriend where couples, lined up in cars, would make out all night.

One day, my mother asked me if I went there and canoodled with my boyfriend. Knowing that I would get in trouble if I told the truth or if I lied, I decided to be honest:

'Oh yes, Mother, passionately!' Because I said it in a sarcastic way, she didn't believe me and thought I was her little angel. Summer never figured out this trick.

Don't:
Do it
yourself.

With it out in the open that Ryan and I were now sexually active teenagers, our sleepovers became much more frequent. He would leave clothes at my house and I always kept a hair straightener and a swimsuit at his. (Priorities.) But sharing a space with someone can be really tough. That's why I decided to ask Donna to trade rooms with me. I mean, since she was single and all, it made much more sense for Ryan and me to have the walk-in closet, private balcony and attached bathroom.

Now, don't think I was salting Donna's game. She truly had no interest in finding a male suitor. You can ask her. She knew that she liked making her own decisions and didn't really want a man stepping in and trying to raise her children (or change the channel).

So, after much pestering, Donna said that I could have her bedroom. She was a little hesitant because she had been watching Dr Phil a lot, and he said that sexually active teens were the devil. (Well, not in those words, but basically ...) Thankfully, Donna was Donna and trusted that I would not make a baby, contract an STI or drop out of school.

I immediately decided that I needed to redecorate. My mom's dated Laura Ashley floral motif was NOT cool. Nope, I wanted a red room. An older girl at school had one, and I was sure that if I had one too, it would make me incredibly happy and undeniably cool. Not to mention, I had just seen Destiny's Child's house on *MTV Cribs*. And if Beyoncé said a dark colour scheme attracted romance, love and artistic energy, then I *knew* that my life would be perfect once I had one too.

Donna was sold on the idea when I announced that I would do all the redecorating work myself. Of course, I promised it would not become another unfinished project, like when I turned my room into a tacky romantic motel suite look-alike. (An unfortunate amount of pink and a queen-sized waterbed were involved in that one. But let's be honest, I was six when that happened and I had clearly matured since then. My new idea was *not* just a fad.) I convinced my mom that all I needed was some paint, brushes, rollers and tape; then I would be satisfied with my room for the rest of my life. So off we went to Home Depot for the supplies.

The minute we got back to the house, I raced upstairs, moved my furniture to the middle of the room and swept up the abundance of crap from under my bed.[9]

Anyway, for the next step in my room remodelling I called Lauren and told her to come over. I put on a holey t-shirt/sweatpants combo and pressed play on my stereo. After an intense two-hour preparation that included dancing around my room to a mix of Tatu, *NSync and Britney, Lauren and I needed recharging. A box of pepperoni

---

9   This crap haul included, but was not limited to: ponytail holders, Corn Pops, some pictures (from when I had my regrettable one-inch-long lesbian secretary haircut) covered in a combination of hair, sand, and syrup from 1996, and a massive (unused) condom collection I started when I was ten. Okay, I'd better explain that one. You see, Brett has always been into skateboarding and used to hang out at a skate/head shop called Smoke. Every time I was in there with Donna to pick him up, I would grab a handful of free condoms because they were colourful. (I especially loved the blue ones with the reservoir tip.) So, really, me hoarding condoms was Brett's fault for hanging out at Smoke so damn much.

Bagel Bites and a gallon of Jolt cola did the trick. I was officially ready.

Lauren took a seat on the floor to watch me work. I picked up a brush dripping with red paint, and thought it would be fun to draw a few things on my stark white walls before I fully transformed the room into the Moroccan fortress of my dreams. First up: a frog. (This is my go-to art.) Then, after getting creative with hearts, I decided to write my name and declare my love for my boyfriend. And finally, with such a great canvas to work with, my inappropriate self could not resist what was about to happen next. It started with the balls, which, of course, gauged what size the shaft was going to be. And as I carefully rounded out the head, I decided that I was pleased with the appendage that I had just painted on my wall. It only needed some final touches: hair, veins and, of course, flying sperm. So, to recap, there was now an eight-foot long, throbbing penis on my wall, surrounded by my name, a frog, some hearts and 'I love Ryan'.

I showed Donna, who was mildly entertained, but told me that I needed to paint over it. Five messy coats later, I was sweating and hyperventilating, with my head between my legs. My artwork was still clear as day. A gigantic cock kept staring at me from my bedroom wall. Even after working into the wee hours of the night, slopping on more and more paint to try and hide my anatomy lesson, it just kept showing through. I also noticed that there was an equal amount of red paint on our wood floors as there was on the actual walls. Time to admit I was in over my head.

Around 6 a.m., I threw in the towel; Donna had to hire painters to fix the 'mess' I had made. Two grown men walked in to cover up the red-light district that my bedroom had become. Awkward silence ensued, as they professionally painted over my 'art' and transformed the walls into a nice, neutral shade of beige. I still tried to be helpful and involved, but making eye contact was nearly impossible.

Come to think of it, pretty much all of my future DIY projects also failed. I always end up spending $100 on craft supplies only to hot-glue my beach shell picture frame to my carpet. (The only thing close to a successful endeavour involved bedazzling some jeans for my ninth-grade entrepreneurship class. I started a Spirit Jeans business that would trick out students' pants for pep rallies and game days. It was going really well until I caught a glimpse of myself wearing them in the mirror. I had literally bedazzled 98 per cent of the surface area of my pants.)

I want nothing more than to craft my heart out. But, after spending an hour on Pinterest, I just know, deep down, that I can't execute. I have since retired from the do-it-yourself industry. Turns out, I work better in the don't-involve-yourself one.

Don't:
Overwork
your party
trick.

Standing out in the world is tough. With so many little Asian prodigies playing classical instruments, and twelve-year-old boys with shoulder-length hair catching twenty feet of air on half-pipe ramps, it's difficult to make your mark. I have tried countless things, such as shovelling tablespoons of cinnamon into my mouth, chugging a two-litre bottle of Coke, and actually attempting to become a real-life contortionist. You're probably wondering how those turned out, so I'll give you a quick summary: after failing, more than a few times, to swallow a mouthful of cinnamon, I have deemed this task to be impossible. However, I *have* chugged a two-litre bottle of Coke and have also been caught with both of my legs behind my head.

We all know someone with a party trick. Sometimes it's the guy funnelling two beers' worth of pool water in three seconds (Brett), or the girl on the dance floor showing off her insane moves (Donna). And, since you know me pretty well by now, you probably assume that I have a party trick. But you'd be wrong: I have *four* (aside from being a blonde Jew). My go-to (outfit-dependent) is doing a split against a wall. The next one (again, outfit-dependent) is doing the Worm. My third is doing a vagina fart on command. (*Much* more on that later.) The fourth, however, has long since been retired due to the extreme risks involved. Don't worry, I'll explain.

The key to having a successful and legendary party trick is *how* the act occurs. First off, if you spontaneously burst into your performance, people may not be primed. They might miss the wow factor. Instead, they'd be too busy assuming (and rightfully so) that you are just the drunk and/or annoying kid, begging for attention. Secondly, if you volunteer the trick yourself, you look like an obnoxiously cocky show-off.

The best route to go is to carefully begin a conversation or suggest a topic that you can manipulate. Then, you subtly steer the discussion in a direction that will lead to a request for your party trick. Once you allude to the fact that you can perform a mind-blowing act of greatness, your audience will beg you for it. Talk it up just enough to make them require you to prove your capabilities. Finally, walk – don't run – to the performance space (that you strategically cleared earlier). Be sure it's an area that's perfect for you to capture the attention of your fellow partygoers.

Your presentation should highlight your most impressive skill. If you're like me, you will usually pull out the flexibility card. My split against the wall works wonders to a) Impress non-flexible people; b) Make boys notice my long and tanned legs which, as the great Cher Horowitz once said, 'Makes them think of sex'; and c) Secure a make-out session with at least one douche bag.

The Worm, on the other hand, gives me a little more credibility. If you can pull it off, it can be classified as breakdancing. More than once, it has gotten me a little chocolate–vanilla swirl make-out action. Oh, and PLEASE do not do either of these acts in a dress. I did once. And, yet again, I had no underwear on. Yes, my tampon string showed. An oversight like this will quickly and permanently void the awesomeness of your trick.

If you look deeper into my closet of retired party tricks, boyfriends and sequined clothing, you will find the fourth trick, a feat as captivating as a unicorn. Not everyone believes that this act can be done, and rarely has anyone seen it. I, however, have the scar to prove it. Please note: what I am about to describe should NOT be attempted at home (unless you're a professional contortionist).

It came about when, in my sixteenth year of life, I discovered a gift. This gift came in the form of a backbend. An extreme backbend. Once I fully made a bridge (feet and hands firmly planted on the ground), my body would 'click' as if a key were unlocking a door. And it ended up unlocking a doorway to greatness. The click happened right in my belly button. And once it did, I was then able to bend even further, putting my chest on the floor. Then, inching my head closer to my feet, my body would take the shape of a circle (imagine a human hula hoop). As spectators would draw closer, I'd take the trick a step further and lick my foot.

This trick wowed crowds up and down the state of Florida. And my act went international when I joined the Spanish Club in 2003. Our trip to Spain seemed like the perfect time to bust it out. Dressed in tight white pants and a red tube top (perfect party-trick attire if you can get past the small outline of a camel toe), I boarded a party boat with my friends off the coast of Barcelona. Aboard this vessel full of caffeine-loaded teenagers, we began to dance like we'd never danced before. The ride was like a field trip on steroids.

Eventually, all of us formed a circle and started playing Love Potion Number 9. (If you're unaware of what this is, it's when one or two people jump in the middle and dance for about thirty seconds.) When it was my turn, I jumped into place, all eyes on me. As the red and blue lights illuminated the dance floor, I rooted my hands and feet to the ground and arched backward. The trick had begun. When in position, I heard the 'click' and knew that I could go even further. Finally, my tongue came in contact with my foot. Eyes wide, I knew I had yet again achieved party-trick SUCCESS!

When I got home from Spain I started to notice something a little weird about my belly button (aka my clicker). It was squishy. Not fat-squishy, but like sac-of-fluid-squishy. I told Ryan's mom, Yvonne, about it. She told me that I probably had a hernia. Her husband (a MASSIVE man) had one. His was the really awkward, visible kind of hernia that pokes through clothing. (You couldn't help but stare.) In fear of being the girl in high school with the golf-ball belly, I entered accelerated, horrified panic mode and quickly arranged to see the doctor. Twenty-four hours later, it was confirmed: my bowels were coming through my abdomen. Every time I heard that 'click', I had actually been hearing my abdominal muscles slowly ripping apart. Time to schedule an operation and get my sac of shit pushed back into its proper compartment.

While anxiously awaiting the operation[10], I decided to get a cute hot-pink knock-off Juicy Couture jumpsuit. The reality show *Newlyweds* was really popular at the time, and I wanted nothing more than to look like Jessica Simpson. When the time came to go under the knife, I donned the head-to-toe, blindingly pink velour and entered the hospital for my outpatient surgery. They did a keyhole operation through my belly button, and that was that.

After I woke up from the anaesthesia and thanked the doctor for putting my poo back where it belonged, I swapped the paper gown for my Pink Panther costume and went on my way. They pushed me outside in a wheelchair and I waited for Donna to pull the car around. Groggy and sore, I looked around and read the sign above the exit: 'Women's Care: Obstetrics and Gynaecology'. Then I noticed that all of the women around me had new babies. Paranoid (because I lived in a small town where word travelled fast), I covered my face with my hair. The last thing I needed was to be recognised; once that happened, it would be a full-on pregnancy rumour. I must have looked like a brand-spanking-new teen mom, and I suddenly started to hate my *Real Housewives of Gainesville* pink beacon of an outfit.

I managed to escape without being spotted, and headed home. Sort of. Since I was sixteen and spent most of my time at Ryan's house, I wanted to be helpless on his couch for as long as possible. After setting up shop on his family's green elbow lounge, I turned on *Finding Nemo*.

---

10 Weird confession: I thoroughly enjoy everything about surgery. All those things you probably hate (hospitals, casts, crutches, wraps, icepacks, braces, bandaids and stitches) only bring me joy, because others will be forced to pay massive amounts of attention to me. Really, anything that will make people feel sorry for me is a win.

My friend Megan came over to take care of me. Megan is one of my best friends in the entire world. I remember when she transferred to Jordan Glen in the eighth grade. I didn't think I'd like her, because I'd considered 'Megan' a mean-girl name. Nope, this Megan turned out to be like a hot, busty, female Chris Farley. And her family was every bit as amazing. Moo, as I liked to call her, brought magazines and cookies and lay on the couch with me for hours.[11]

After some quality girl time, Megan waved goodbye and said she'd be back the next day. I flipped through a *Cosmo* magazine and discovered fifty-two new ways to please my man, but couldn't stop thinking about the fact that I hadn't pooped all day long. I was convinced that I was constipated, since my standard was two bowel movements a day and that wasn't happening. I started chasing my pain-killers with a little Metamucil. Ten hours later, I needed to poop. Right away. The unforeseen issue: I couldn't really walk or sit on my own. If only Megan was still there to help!

So this became the first time that I shat in front of a significant other. Ryan was kind enough to help me walk to the toilet and get situated. Unfortunately, he was also kind enough to stay until I finished. Have you ever leaned against a significant other while you took a poop? It's not exactly the most comfortable thing (physically or emotionally) to do. But Metamucil made it both possible and a little bit unavoidable.

Trips to the hospital and toilet problems aside, I still really love doing party tricks. You will always be able to

---

11   At one point we talked about her super-possessive Colombian boyfriend, Jesus, who had recently pissed off her dad, Roger. Megan had *just* gotten a BMW 3 Series and Jesus decided to 'pimp her ride'. He did this by adding subwoofers and two amplifiers to her stereo. He also hung a Colombian flag from the rear-view mirror and bedazzled the shit out of her licence plate. It was hysterical to see a nice white Catholic girl cruise around in her pimped-out Beamer.

find me whipping out the Worm in a public setting, and I'm still probably the only girl who practises jumping up from being on her back to her feet (just in case I really need to wow someone). Party tricks are simply a part of who I am. And if they weren't incorporated into my social life, I don't really know who I would be. I mean, what other skills do I have, really? I can't cure cancer and can't talk about politics without sounding incredibly uninformed. All I have is my bendy body and my impeccable timing. If you got it, flaunt it, right? Just make sure you're wearing the correct attire. And that you're not ripping your abdominal wall.

Don't:
Use shampoo
as a
lubricant.

A great opportunity to showcase your party trick is on spring break. If you grew up in north-central Florida, you will know all about St Augustine Beach. It's frequented by equal proportions of redneck and affluent Floridians who are all looking for the same things: beach, booze and bungalows. I felt like I'd hit the jackpot when I discovered that Ryan's family had a beach house there. I *knew* I'd hit the jackpot when his very trusting parents let us go to the house on our own one weekend. What we didn't mention to them about this weekend was that we were going to bring all of our friends. In other words, me and twenty other eager-to-get-drunk-and-fornicate teens gathered up some tequila, rum, vodka, beer and various drugs, then took off on an adventure worthy of a Cancún spring break.

Before getting there, we had to stop by the property manager's place to pick up the key. Once we got into the bungalow, we promptly situated ourselves around the kitchen table to play drinking games. Approximately half of the alcohol we were trying to consume ended up on the floor and the table, creating an interesting brownish glue-like substance. It wasn't long until we broke out the beer funnel and began accelerating our inebriation. The rate that we were peeing at was ridiculous and, on my seventeenth journey to the toilet, I broke the handle. The ounce of responsibility that was still inside of me took the broken piece and made a mental note to repair it before we left. For the moment, we'd just leave the back off and manually flush our alcoholic urine and beer poops.

The rest of the first night actually went relatively smoothly. The boys took shots of Bacardi 151 while the girls played Never Have I Ever in an effort to let everyone know how slutty and badass we were. Only one person vomited (you know, 'that guy'), and everyone was in bed by a respectable 4 a.m. The next day was spent playing on the beach, swimming and cracking open the first beer at noon. But then came the second night, which took a turn for the worse.

Now, I'm not entirely clear on the events that took place between the hours of 8 p.m. and 9 a.m., but I do know that whatever happened was extremely fucked up. All I can say for sure is that I was dreaming about drinking water and eating watermelon when I woke up on the couch, wrapped in Ryan's arms. There were about nine bodies on the floor around us, generating a steady hum of snoring and the usual amount of drool. I carefully got up and walked to the sink. Having no time for a glass, I simply bent over, stuck my head under the tap and gulped some much-needed H_2O. Feeling somewhat better, I surveyed the damage. We had a sticky, mud-caked floor and a bench littered with red cups. Wet towels and sand were everywhere, along with some scattered Cheetos and the remnants of a pizza. The trash can was overflowing, and we had left the freezer open all night. In the bathroom, I found the shower curtain torn down, the toilet broken (my bad) and the distinct smell of urine.

But all that damage was nothing compared to what I saw after walking into the master bedroom. The bed had been moved to the middle of the room, and there were four bodies lying, in a lifeless manner, across it. And there was blood. A lot of blood. It was mixed with shampoo and conditioner, which was everywhere. After I checked pulses and screamed at the hung-over bodies to explain what had happened, I was informed that one couple had needed some lubrication during their lovemaking session. Naturally, they thought shampoo and conditioner would be good options. I was also told that the female counterpart had gotten a small cut in her vagina and it would not stop bleeding. So there I was, in someone else's house, having to deal with a massive vagina blood–and–hair care product situation.

Trying to be a responsible teenager, I woke everyone up to clean house. Ryan needed to leave for a tennis tournament, so I was in charge. Ryan explained that he would return the key to the property manager on his way out, and the door would lock behind us. With that, we kissed goodbye. Of course, some of our friends went with him, and a few more went to the beach. All in all, one girl stayed behind to help me clean up the bloody mess. So much for a team effort.

Thing is, I actually really enjoy cleaning up after a bender. It feels so good to take out the trash, wipe the counters, mop the floors and get rid of the vomit left behind by 'that guy'. Everything was going really well. With massive full garbage bags multiplying by the door, it was time to make a trash run. The two of us were contentedly walking to the dumpster when we heard the door shut. The door had locked behind us and, in our hung-over state, we had forgotten that we didn't have a key to get back in! Commence full-on freak out.

The first thing my mind flashed to was the lovely master bedroom that my friends had turned into the set of a snuff film. We hadn't gotten around to cleaning that mess yet. So, in a panic, the two of us attempted to get back in by any means possible. We tried the back doors, the windows and even picking the lock. Nothing. I called Ryan to explain, but there was no way he could come back to get the key. To make matters worse, his father was coming in a couple of hours to stay for the week.

There was no other choice but to leave. We had made our (bloody) beds and now we had to lie in them. Luckily, I had my car keys in my pocket (how they got there, I will never know), so we were off. Driving home was nerve-racking, since the only thing I could think of was the impending phone call of doom. At twenty past twelve, my cell rang. I turned down 50 Cent and picked up. Predictably, it was Ryan's dad, and he wanted answers to the following questions:

How many people were actually at his house?
What did we do to his toilet?
Where was the handle?
Why were there bottles of shampoo and conditioner next to his bed?
Why was his bed in the middle of the room?
Why was there blood everywhere?
Did we sacrifice a small animal?
Was there an illegal abortion?

Who left the freezer open?
Did I plan on buying him any replacement Hungry Man Frozen Dinners?
Were we *really* that dumb?

I wasn't quite able to answer most of those questions (at least, not comfortably). My main goal was to assure him that I was definitely *not* that dumb and that one of Ryan's low-life friends was totally responsible for the crime scene. I also promised that I'd never do anything so destructive again.

To my knowledge, I've pretty much kept that promise. It's okay to bleed all over your own room, but not someone else's. Words to live by.

LESSONS LEARNT IN YOUR TWENTIES (OR, IN MY CASE, EARLY TEENS)

Even though Donna is super-trusting, and a very accepting parent, she definitely didn't love my newfound desire to party. She had already been through her fair share: I shaved my legs at age nine, wore a water bra at ten and pierced my belly button at thirteen. I was, in short, on a mission to experience experiences. After a heated debate in seventh grade on whether I could get my tongue pierced or not, she asked, 'If everyone was jumping off a bridge, would you do it too?' I responded, honestly, 'Yes.'

Do: Fake it till you make it (to twenty-one).

The summer after Laura and I went to the Bahamas, Ryan, Sarah, Brett and I decided that we all wanted fake IDs. As we were always (usually) honest with Mama Donna, Brett and I told her that we each needed $60 to buy some. We supported our argument by stating that we loved to dance and needed them to get in to nightclubs. Donna wasn't that shocked, but she immediately asked us why, in that case, we couldn't just be eighteen on our new IDs. But we quickly shot her down, claiming that all of the good 'dancing' venues were twenty-one[1] and up.

In no time, we were on our way to a seedy apartment complex in a not-so-nice part of town. Once we arrived at the home of the ID-maker, we knocked on the door and waited impatiently. After about thirty seconds of painting a mental picture of my new ID and imagining myself wearing tight white pants and a glittery top at the coolest club, a guy who looked like a seventh-year college senior opened the door. He led us inside, made sure we had our money and explained how the process was going to work: we had to pick a state other than Florida for our new identities, because it was too hard to duplicate Florida's hologram. I chose Mississippi, which made Biloxi my new hometown. I was stoked. Not only did I get a fake ID, but I also got to have a fake accent that took me one step closer to sounding like Britney Spears.

Summer Land from Biloxi did me proud. For our first outing with our new IDs we decided to go to a club downtown called Eden. Sarah and I went shopping for the perfect club wear. I settled on tight white pants, a sparkly blue top and a 'diamond' necklace. Sarah wore black pants and a

---

1   How lame is the US with its drinking age of twenty-one? Also, why can we drive when we're sixteen? Donna thinks twelve-year-olds are way more level-headed than hormone-fuelled teenagers. Agreed.

beaded maroon tube top that came down to a point right at her belly button. Unlike previous nights, we were all dressed up with somewhere to go.

We arrived at Eden around 10.30 and had to wait in line. When we finally got to the bouncer (some twenty-something college student who clearly loved the gym and protein shakes too much), we all figuratively shat ourselves as he shone the black light over the holograms. He must have had bigger concerns (like working on his tan the next morning) because he happily let us through the door: 'Have a good night.'

THANK GOD.

To be fair to the bouncer, we didn't actually look that young. Even though I was just fourteen, I had this awkwardly mature short haircut that really did make me look like a responsible 21-year-old. And with all of the make-up we were wearing, I'm pretty sure twelve-year-olds were indistinguishable from thirty-year-olds in those days.

We were officially 'clubbing'. Turned out clubbing wasn't all that exciting. My pants were almost instantly black and covered in man sweat, vodka tonics and an excessive amount of bronzer. But the story I told at school the next week made everything worth it. I was cool. Like, fake ID–carrying cool.

In high school, my fake ID was more of a novelty. It was a huge popularity booster at parties when I'd take it out and show people. Since the majority of the people I was friends with didn't have fake IDs, I only sporadically went to clubs. I did, however, buy beer and spray paint, all in all getting my mom's money's worth out of it.

Don't:
Leave a
paper trail.

That fake ID also allowed me into the world of body art, which got me into an awkward situation. Multiple times. Have you ever been self-conscious because you have a zodiac tattoo on your lower stomach that looks like a sperm? I have. When I was sixteen, I decided that I wanted to get a tattoo of the Leo zodiac symbol because my dad and I are both Leos. I felt like I wanted a daily reminder that he was with me in spirit. (Well, not with me when I was binge drinking, making out or lying to Donna but, all in all, watching over me.)

Within a week, I loathed that tattoo because it looked like a swimmer that was fresh out of someone's testicles. As the months passed, I started to *really* not stand the fact that it was a ZODIAC TATTOO and began the process of having it lasered off. A decently painful process, especially when you refuse the anaesthetic. Am I just that badass? Not really. I normally get my sperm art numbed before they take the machine to it. But on my third appointment a former classmate, who is now a nurse, was in charge of administering the anaesthetic.

This girl is painfully perfect, and she will let you (and all of her closest 2437 friends on Facebook) know it. In an effort not to reveal my unfortunate tat to her (to avoid being the subject of some nasty gossip), I nervously declined the anaesthetic shots: 'Uh, no, I don't need to get it numbed.'

The doctors came in and commented on how brave I was, going without anaesthetic. Then, protective glasses on, they began to shoot my delicate skin with the laser. As I smelled my skin burning, a nice sharp pain shot up my spine. I commenced deep breathing and mental self-laceration for not getting it numbed.

Everyone in the room was so impressed by my pain threshold (including me) that, the next time I came in, they were like, 'Oh hey, Ms No Anaesthesia!' and I couldn't bring myself to tell them that I actually wanted to have it numbed from that point forward. I also kind of liked the recognition of being such a badass, so I continued, sans pain meds. (Not surprising, I guess. We've clearly established the things I will do for a little attention.)

Sadly, though, the sperm tat is only the most glaring of misjudgements. The pathetic thing is that I actually have an entire *series* of unfortunate tattoos. And it all started at the undeniably mature age of fourteen. To be fair, I was only a month off turning fifteen, but still. Laura and I were summering at her house on Martha's Vineyard and I had that brand-spanking-new fake ID just begging to be used. With card in hand, Summer Land was suddenly seven years older. (She looked stunning for her age.) And since we had been telling our island friends that we were much older than we actually were, I was thrilled to have hard (fake) evidence.

One sunny day, we were all lying by the water, nursing our Nantucket Nectar Cranberry Juice–and–vodka hang-overs and discussing tattoos. An older girl named Christina had just gotten paw prints inked up her thigh, and another had a four-leaf clover stamped on her butt. I started think-ing that this might be the perfect way to start building my wannabe-badass prep-school reputation. Impulsively, we picked our sandy bodies up off the beach and piled into

Christina's grandmother's station wagon to go get me inked! I was confident that my personal stock was about to skyrocket, not only on Martha's Vineyard but also back at school; tenth grade was going to be so much better if I started the year off with a fresh tat.

The entire way to the tattoo parlour, I tried to memorise the information on my fake ID and perfect my Southern drawl. By the time we got to our destination, I realised that I had been so preoccupied with learning my details and anticipating any ID questions that might come up (you never know who might test you by asking if you're a rat or a chicken, according to the Chinese zodiac) that I hadn't taken time to think of what I wanted tattooed on my body *forever*. So I walked in to the parlour and just picked a nice flower design from a poster on the wall. It had daisies in it, and I liked daisies.

Obviously, this was not a well-thought-out plan. But I had to act quickly, because I was intimidated and wanted the artist to think I knew what I was doing. When I handed him my ID I was shaking a little, inside. He then asked for backup because, clearly, I was a child. So I handed over a Visa card (it was for emergencies … and this was clearly an emergency) with my name on it. (The more I think about it, this was all Donna's fault.) After a quick glance to verify my age, my pants were at my ankles and I was face down with a needle to my lower back.

After that, time seemed to speed up and my vacation was over. I had only been home a few days when I found myself at a Japanese steakhouse with Donna, Ryan and his family to celebrate my fifteenth birthday and the start of tenth grade. Almost everyone at the table knew about the tattoo (yes, even Ryan's parents and little brother), but we had kept Donna in the dark. Right after the chef set fire to an onion volcano, my mom said, 'Honey, I've been meaning to ask you – what is this credit card charge from a tattoo parlour on Martha's Vineyard?'

The flames from the table felt like they were foreshadowing my fiery death. Ryan choked on his fried rice, and his mom grabbed my thigh. The jig was up. (How was I supposed to know that my mom actually looked at her credit card statement?) So I told her and braced for the worst, but she wasn't mad at all. Donna is very accepting, and she ended up supporting my act of expression. But she still had to do her motherly duty and teach me a very important lesson: the next time I did something illegal, I needed to withdraw cash first.

With so many things getting a little out of control in my life, I decided to take control. Well, kind of. As a little kid, I was never shy about exploring my body. When I was still young enough to have car-seat status, my mom once opened the sliding door of our Dodge Caravan and found me, my OshKosh B'Gosh overalls unclipped and my legs spread, with my hands in my nani. She said that I was smiling so hard as I asked, 'Do you have one of these? It feels so good!'

Look, we've all been caught pleasuring ourselves at some point. I'm just happy that it happened when I was two and it was 'perfectly natural'. As I grew up, I began to realise that body pillows and stuffed animals were invented for one thing: childhood masturbation. Without these cushy things, what would us girls have to jam between our adolescent thighs, rub up against, and use to experience that heartbeat in our vaginas? Honestly, how else would we know what to look forward to?

Even though I'd had many trysts with my pillow, my first real memory of the big O is from when I was twelve. A bunch of my friends had gotten really into horseback riding. I loved the velvet hats and decided that I wanted to wear a rich-kid costume, too. After twenty minutes of getting comfortable on the horse in my first lesson, it was finally revealed to me why everyone was so willing to spend $50,000 on a fine new steed. Posting. Oh, posting. OOHHHH OHHHH POSTING.

You see, my instructor explained that I was to rub my lower region on this finely polished genuine leather saddle, and then push off the seat and up in the air, repeatedly. And of course, this was done rhythmically with the gait of the horse. It took me all of five seconds to realise that I needed to own a horse. So I set off on this mission, in a manner similar to Veruca Salt: 'I want a golden horse, Mommy, and I want it now!'

True to form, Donna supported yet another one of my 'I swear to god I am going to do this for the rest of my life' hobbies and purchased a horse. She was a white Arabian named Bint Bint Rodeen, and she was to help me in my effort to become the competitive rider I promised my mom I would be. She was beautiful. She was also dangerously aloof and skittish. (Just the thing I needed to explore my sexuality.)

But after nearly rubbing my clit off and falling off her numerous times, I wasn't so keen on Bint Bint anymore. Not to mention, I was (and am) obnoxiously ADHD and got bored with horseback riding (and myself) after about six months. So, with that, my mom sold her when I was away at summer camp. By that point, I was busy practising making out with my friends, so moving on was relatively easy. Still, to this day, I can't look at a horse without feeling nostalgic.

To be honest, I can't look at a tub of vaseline the same way, either. It's because of the part it played in the first time I (intentionally) masturbated. It started with a steamy hot shower, to help me relax. Then, I lit some candles and rubbed lotion all over my body. Once under the covers, I slid my hand down my Abercrombie & Fitch Christmas moose–patterned pyjama pants and started to explore.

Although I was not lacking any lubrication, I had heard about K-Y Jelly and figured that it could only enhance this amazing feeling. Only problem: I didn't have any. Hmmm, but did I have a suitable substitute? Suddenly, I remembered that my mom had a tub of vaseline. So I took a brief break from my self-lovemaking session and went to raid her supply. After finding what I needed, I excitedly got back in bed. With a load of vaseline globbed onto my finger, I was ready to go down south again.

As it turns out, VASELINE IS NOT A LUBRICANT THAT SHOULD BE USED ON YOUR VAGINA. This petroleum substance ended up clumping down there and basically suffocated my hole. Both of my flaps were drawn to each other as if one were a magnet and the other were steel. (Such a good song.)

Feeling moderately panicked, I got in the shower to wash it off. But it also turns out that vaseline is decidedly water-resistant. I watched the H_2O roll off the surface of my skin while I tried to use my stubby nails to scrape off the anti-sex lube. After a valiant effort, I shut off the shower, dried myself and went to bed. I hoped that a good night's sleep would take care of everything.

I woke up with thrush.

Don't worry. I eventually learned how to pleasure myself right. Turns out that I didn't need candles, lube or even a hot steamy shower. All it took was an episode of *Sex and the City* (or a Boston crime movie) and my pillow. Everything was right there in bed with me, all along. I was just too blind to see. Kind of romantic, if you think about it.

Do:
Drop out
of school.

Since I'd spent eight years at Jordan Glen – that magical hippie school with peacocks, ducks and chickens – it may come as no surprise that I did not adjust well to public (non-hippie) school. Going from an entire grade of nine kids to one of nine hundred really threw off the balance of my chi. My teachers were no longer on a first-name basis with me. Jeff and Sally became Mrs I-Hate-My-Job and Mr I-Take-Myself-Too-Seriously. On top of all that, I was now summoned by a bell and needed to obtain a hall pass just to use the restroom. Since when did I need permission to urinate?

In the beginning, I really did try to like school. But my prison sentence (aka time on Aviance) was really bringing me down. I felt like I had NO time for friends, my boyfriend or drinking. I finally realised what was going to make my time at Buchholz bearable: being a cheerleader. And not just any cheerleader – a football cheerleader[2]. Toward the end of ninth grade, I quit Aviance and decided to try out for the cheerleading squad.

I was a seasoned dancer, having taken classes since I was three, but I was sure that I'd need to enlist the help of some experienced girls to help me master my back hand-spring and jaw-breaking smile for tryouts. Then I'd need to combo that with a good winky face ;). Every day, during sixth period, Andrea and Frannie spotted me while I tried to hone the art of gymnastics.

This came rather easily, as one of my alter egos is a tiny Romanian gymnast. Her name is Christina Lachee, and she has been in my life since I was about eleven. She mostly comes out when I hurl my body around in the living room, do somersaults through the kitchen, and during my backbend. She always makes sure I stick the landing, with my butt clenched, arms held in a high V and a sharp head pop at the end. You've got to love her dedication to perfection.

With the help of Andrea, Frannie and Christina, I nailed tryouts and became a bona fide cheerleader at the end of the year. Before I knew it, tenth grade had arrived and I was a brand-new member of the cheer squad. I could hardly sleep the night before the first pep rally. Since that stupid school started at stupid o'clock, I woke up at 5.45 a.m. to make sure I looked flawless in my not-so-dress-code-appropriate cheer uniform, complete with a yellow glitter ribbon tied in a bow around my ponytail.

---

2 There are three religions in the southern US: Methodist, Baptist and Football. Cheering for a football team is a huge deal. Even for Jewish girls.

Just like every great teen movie featuring a slow-motion hallway walk, the sea of students parted as I strolled through them in a manner similar to Kate Moss. (Kate Moss in a cheerleading uniform, mind you.) By lunch, even my ego had developed its own cheer squad.

When I saw Ryan standing in line to get pizza at lunch, I giddily trotted over to greet him and hang off his arm. A bunch of kids started yelling that I was skipping the line, and the lunch lady yelled at me to go to the back of the line. Seeing as I wasn't even going to order food anyway, I thought that the appropriate response was to say 'Fuck that!' and walk away. Feisty, eh?

Apparently, my sassiness wasn't universally admired, as I was reported to the principal for calling the lunch lady a 'fat bitch'. Which I didn't! I said 'Fuck that!' Of course, Donna was called in to figure out my punishment. Unluckily for the dean, my mom believed me. She kept trying to explain my story, that I hadn't called Ms Lunch Lady a 'fat bitch', but rather that I had simply said 'fuck that', which was completely different and totally acceptable. The dean rebutted with, '"Fuck that" is not acceptable either.' This went on for a while.

By the time we had all collectively said 'fuck that' about a dozen times, there was steam coming out of the dean's ears. I tried to defend myself by explaining that Donna was fat, and that I am not heartless enough to call anyone a 'fat bitch', because 'I'm sensitive to that kind of shit'. Of course, that argument failed, and I was sent home with two days of in-school suspension.

As it turned out, I *loved* in-school suspensions. You didn't have to go to any of your classes, and you got to sit in the auditorium with all of the other rebels. All you did was easy worksheets to pass the time. And I *loved* worksheets.

At the end of the day, when my peers passed in about five sheets, I sauntered up to our supervisor and turned in about fifty. Such an overachiever.

When I finished my days of suspension, I went back to class as usual. Not long afterwards, a bunch of us were standing in the hallway, waiting for our teacher to come and unlock the locker room door after our third-period phys. ed. class ended. We needed to get in to the locker room and change out of our sweaty clothes, which (for us hormonal teens with smelly pits) was a time-sensitive problem. So, naturally, I started rattling the door. On my final push forward, it flew open and I started laughing.

A girl named Latavia started mocking my laugh. I playfully giggled, 'Shut up' and kept laughing. Suddenly, Latavia was in my face, screaming, 'Was there a change in weather?! This white girl did NOT just tell me to shut up! Say it again and I will bust your face in!'

Little white Summer was scared shitless. I did not want to get my ass handed to me by some cheeky chick. Plus, I was really worried about my face. I loved my face. I loved everything, from my uneven nostrils to my slightly-too-high nose bridge to my freckle (okay, fine, it's a mole) above my lip. The very thought of Latavia damaging what Donna gave me was enough for me to go home from school and NEVER return. Literally. I went home and told Donna that it was simply not safe there, and that homeschooling was the only option. I briefly mourned the fact that I would no longer get to wear my cheerleading uniform, but enough was enough. I had to get out of there.

To be honest, I'd gotten the idea from Megan, who was also having a hard time in the public school system. These dickhead soccer dudes relentlessly called her Pat because of her short, boylike haircut (Pat being the androgynous character from *Saturday Night Live*). On top of the taunts, the same guys would twist ketchup packets and throw them at her feet. After a year of ketchup-caked jeans, she told her mom, Sally, that she was too rich and too nice to be treated that way and needed to be homeschooled immediately.

So, at the start of the second semester of tenth grade, we began taking correspondence classes through an accredited national program. We dubbed our alternative-learning program Jolly Times Academy. The benefits were immediate. Megan and I would meet every morning at Starbucks (the handicap tables make the perfect desks) to do our work. This was followed by lunch and our joint tennis lesson at Gainesville Country Club. For more challenging subjects, like Spanish and math, we met with our tutors. It all made us feel just like child actors. (And, at that point in my life, I would have done just about anything to be one step closer to a life like Hilary Duff's.) Roger, Megan's dad, would take us on 'educational' field trips to places like Universal Studio's Islands of Adventure. This helped us broaden our knowledge of the Jurassic period and the legend of Sinbad. You know, all the crucial things that teenagers need to know.

By eleventh grade, we qualified to dual-enrol at our local community college (which meant we took college classes, but they counted as high school, too). It was great, because we could enrol in 'name only' through our high schools, and they would pay for all of our college textbooks and classes.

Megan and I much preferred the new college schedule to the alternative. Classes starting at 10 a.m. were so much more manageable, and allowed us to keep up with our weekly breakfast dates at the 43rd Street Deli. Starting the day with poached eggs and hash browns was way better than a school bell.

Do:
Be a star.

The only downside to our new schedule was that we couldn't set foot on our high school campus. Like, ever. Not only could we not visit at lunch, but we needed SPECIAL PERMISSION to go to prom. I know it was premature, but I had already purchased three prom dresses. I had been looking forward to prom since I was just a wee little foetus. Since I hadn't been the most popular girl in high school, I didn't expect to be prom queen or anything. No, I just wanted to get all dressed up in my purple satin strapless gown, take photos by someone's pool, ride in a limo and sneak alcohol all night.

Turned out, my plan was about to be derailed. While I was busy with my alternative education, Ryan was busy talking up other girls at school. Not that I could blame him. Our relationship had started to deteriorate after we went to a Britney Spears concert together.

While at the concert, I was approached by someone who told me I should be a model. Seeing as my main goal in life was to achieve ultimate stardom and be ridiculously cool, this flattery was more than welcomed! The woman explained that she was a model and talent scout. Now, normally, Britney Spears is all consuming. However, at this particular concert, I couldn't stop thinking about myself and how much of a star I was going to be. Every time Britney purred one of her lyrics, I got more and more entranced by the idea of me being just as super-famous. As soon as Monday rolled around, I called to get more information.

The perky scout at John Robert Powers told me that I had major star potential and set up a meeting at their office in Jacksonville for the next day. The question that I didn't know to ask was 'How much?' In the morning, my mom and I drove over to meet with Kim of John Robert Powers. I performed a monologue for her and took some photos. She explained that I really had raw talent, but that a great performer must always work on her craft.

Kim went into detail about all of the classes I should be taking. Runway, Acting 1, Improv and Interview Skills. I was a little sceptical, but blinded by my desire to be famous. I looked around the walls of her office and saw so many recognisable stars who had all gotten their start there. When Kim told me that a year of classes and a trip to LA to showcase my talent at IMTA (International Model and Talent Association) would only cost me $6000, I took one more look at the poster of Josh Duhamel and said, 'Sign me up!!!'

Because it was such a large investment, I took it really seriously. I drove to and from Jacksonville every single day to take my classes and perform for casting directors. At the classes I made some really good friends. Together we would fantasise about our lives in Hollywood and declare that we'd 'never forget each other' if one of us made it first.

It didn't take long for Ryan to be officially placed on the backburner. I don't know if it was because I was exhausted after driving a three-hour round trip every day, or that I was just too lost in my own little dream world, but he was not a priority.

The fact that I wanted to move to Los Angeles in January didn't help either. Lucky for me, I had enough credits to graduate high school early and hit the road. Ryan was sad, but I was just anxious to start the rest of my life. The last six months of our relationship consisted of Ryan hooking up with other girls behind my back, and me subconsciously sabotaging us to make it easier for me to leave. I loved him, but my life in Hollywood was waiting for me.

Right after I finished my last high school classes, Donna and I packed my car and put it on a truck bound for Los Angeles. I boarded a flight the next day and was off to become the next Goldie Hawn, moving in with some fellow John Robert Powers wannabe actors and beginning the quest for fame.

The first few months in LA were incredibly exciting, but hard. I didn't have my boyfriend to confide in anymore. What made matters worse was finding out that Ryan got a new girlfriend just eleven days after I left. (Lauren had learned this from the new girlfriend's Xanga page. Burn.) I don't know why he kept it from me, but the lie actually hurt more than the actual fact. The only thing that made matters worse was that they were going to prom. TOGETHER.

Living in LA as a seventeen-year-old without your parents is difficult. My skin was definitely not thick enough, no matter how much I tried to convince myself that it was. I went on auditions and took acting classes every week.

I even tried to lose weight so that I would be camera-ready. My roommate was really into Slim-Fast shakes. I would try to only have one for breakfast, but was still starving by 10 a.m. and would cave in for a Full English. To say that diet failed is an understatement.

By month five, I had to face facts and accept that I just wasn't as good as the other hopefuls out there. I wasn't super-skinny. I couldn't cry on command, and I sure as hell couldn't fake a German accent to save my life.

Not long after that, I decided that I was not ready for casting couches, cocaine, nipple pasties or extremely bitchy girls, so I applied to Emerson College in Boston. So much for the whole 'never giving up in LA' promise to myself. For someone whose main dream in life was achieving ultimate stardom and being cool, this was essentially the end of the world.

I decided to fly home for the month of May. I needed Donna. Badly. I knew that being alone in LA on prom night was only going to make me feel like more of a reject.

I was sitting in my living room with Sarah, eating out of a box of a dozen Krispy Kreme donuts (the 'HOT' sign was on …) and watching a marathon of *The O.C.* when Brett called and asked what we were doing that night. PROM NIGHT. Tragically, we answered, 'Nothing.'

'How about you two come to a monster-truck rally with us?'

With literally nothing better to do than binge eat and curse the fact that Ryan and Marissa could not sort their shit out, we got up, wiped the doughnut icing from our mouths and went to get dressed for the rally. Brett, Skylar, Jesse, Sarah and I all got in Jesse's red pickup truck and headed to the track. We stopped off at a Wendy's so that we could get some Frosties and French fries. It wasn't exactly on a par with the catered dance event going on at my old high school, but the square burgers, deep-fried potatoes and chocolate ice-cream really did rock my world. I think that was when I started self-medicating with food. (It only took me thirteen kilos and eight stretch marks to make me start channelling my anxiety into exercise.)

Once we got to the rally, we watched as a giant green and black truck with the name Grave Digger ploughed over a row of twenty cars. After some trick bikes flew around the track, I decided to get up and take a walk around. Skylar and Brett were thoroughly entertained by the cars, and Jesse and Sarah were entertained by each other. Feeling like the fifth wheel, I decided to sign up for a chin-up competition at a US Army promo stand. Only problem: I couldn't do a chin-up to save my life. Instead, they just had me hang in the 'up' position for as long as possible. I won a keychain. As I watched the wife beater–clad men around me laugh and holler while chugging their Budweisers, I started to miss Ryan. I don't know if it was because he was a little bit redneck or I was just feeling isolated, but I definitely felt sad that I wasn't at prom with him.

I went home, put on my saddest emo music and cried. For hours. I broke all of the blood vessels in my eyes and more or less just ate the snot that was streaming from my nose. I was so angry that I was back where I'd started. But this time I had no boyfriend, no acting reel and no hope. I looked up at a picture of me and Ryan hanging on my wall and slammed my fist into it. Blood trickled down my hand as the glass worked its way into my hideous blue carpet. It was all very dramatic.

Instead of leaving for LA and never looking back, I'd just about broken my neck trying to get back to where I'd started. Los Angeles was supposed to have been my future, but instead of making all of my dreams come true, LA had pulled a Ryan and shat all over my spirit.

Don't: Worry.

A couple of summers later, life had continued. I was finally over Ryan and my time in LA and was optimistic about my future. Out of the blue, it was brought to my attention that a certain someone was badmouthing me on *The Tonight Show with Jay Leno*. I found this incredibly distasteful, because when I moved to Los Angeles, Donna told me to never talk badly about anyone on a talk show; it was a negative move and one should always be positive. (Advice to live by.)

The person who was breaking this golden rule turned out to be my ex-roommate from LA (who, through a small part in a streak of insanely successful vampire movies, managed to get a spot on Jay Leno). She was talking about her start in Hollywood.

The story started with how she 'moved in with two crazy people' and that 'the girl roommate was delusional. She would buy Tiffany earrings instead of lunch.'

OKAY. First of all, what seventeen-year-old girl who moves to LA isn't delusional? Also, what would a seventeen-year-old Jewish girl be without her Tiffany jewellery? I can also state (regretfully) that, despite her claim, I never missed a meal. As you may recall, I was incredibly depressed in LA and ate my body weight in In-N-Out Burger every day. I also always got the three-for-one deal on cookies at Subway. This girl was *hongray*! When I got to Boston, I was twice my normal size. Not a good look for me.

I don't understand why this ex-roommate couldn't have said something like, 'Yeah, I moved in with another girl who was trying to find work in LA, but she left after five months to go to Emerson College in Boston – which I believe is your alma mater, Jay Leno!' (See how a little research on Wikipedia makes you seem smarter?)

Despite this, I was happy for the ex-roommate and her success. I was also, admittedly, incredibly jealous and wondered what would have happened if I had stayed in LA. Would I still being smoking herbal refreshments with the drummer of a popular punk rock band? Would a certain well-known stand-up comic still be asking girls in front of the Comedy Store to 'get on their knees'? Would I be the star of my own smash-hit sitcom and dubbed America's Sweetheart? I guess we'll never know.

But, whether it was for better or for worse, life went on and I managed to find myself on a different path. I decided that I needed to focus on my education and move on from that crazy little world (which I had desperately wanted to be in).

Do:
Pee before
(and after)
sex.

So I was back in Gainesville with my tail between my legs, waiting for my first term to start at Emerson. When Laura invited me to come live with her and her family on Martha's Vineyard for the summer, I felt like I had finally found an escape.

There is nothing quite like Martha's Vineyard. Only accessible by water or air, this island features beautiful New England–style shingled homes, cobblestoned sidewalks and the best lobster rolls you'll ever have. This particular summer was one of friendship, fermented beverages and serious flirtations. I reconnected with a boy called Charles, who I had flirted with during the previous two summers I'd visited. Charles was from a well-to-do family with a gorgeous home right in Edgartown. His living-room walls were filled with pictures of him playing tennis, heli-skiing, sailing, travelling around Asia and, of course, graduating from prep school. Obviously his WASP credentials were like catnip to this preppy Southern belle. If only he had been Jewish, too.

We were on the island for two months. And two months in 'teenage summer love' years is equivalent to a solid five-year relationship. It was official: I was in Like. I was also in horrific pain, unlike ever before. You know the feeling where you suddenly have to piss like a pregnant woman, but only a tiny (scalding hot) needle (from hell) of urine pokes through your urethra when you actually make it to the toilet? I do.

You see, I had a raging urinary tract infection (UTI). (Not to be confused with a UPI: Unidentified Party Injury.) It felt like I was dry-heaving from my pee hole every time I'd sit down to use the toilet. Naturally, I had been avoiding sex with my ever-so-serious July–August boyfriend for a couple of days and was running out of excuses. Finally, I got some antibiotics and an amazing medicine called AZO Standard, which makes your pee fluorescent orange. But, of course, I still needed to go every thirty seconds.

With that in mind, I am not sure why I thought that it would be a good idea to go on a road trip. But a bunch of us (including Charles) decided to head up to Gay Head[3] for the afternoon. At one point during the ride, I had to pee. *Immediately.* So we pulled over in a tiny town. While Charles loaded up on snacks and refreshments, I clasped Laura's hand and told her that I was about to bust.

It felt like my skin was not strong enough to stay together. If I didn't get to relax my pelvic floor muscles in the next forty-five seconds, the skin between my vagina and

---

3   The Gay Head cliffs are located in Aquinnah, Massachusetts. I still can't say it without giggling like a little kid.

anus was going to tear. My muscles were clenching tighter and tighter as I frantically asked every vendor for a rest room. Up until that day, I had been unaware that vaginal charley horses were actually a real thing. I dare you to pair that with a UTI.

After hearing 'I am so sorry, we do not have a public rest room' countless times, we were directed to the town hall. It was only a block or two away, but it felt like the last leg of a marathon. Laura and I ran the whole way. Somehow I made it to the bathroom and into the stall (no time to shut the door) without peeing myself. You'd think that I would have been relieved. Nope.

As my fingers fumbled with my zipper, I screamed, 'I can't get my pants undone, I can't get my pants undone!' Then the two of us watched, in horror, as fluorescent-orange urine began to bleed through my light khaki pants. (Actually, *Laura's* light khaki pants that I was borrowing. My bad.) We stared as it trickled down my thighs, burning my freshly shaven legs. Afterwards, I tried to clean myself up as best I could, but the orange dye in the medicine was clinging to the fabric tighter than a Jewish mother. It simply was not coming off. (Laura offered to lend me some other shorts, but they didn't fit. Living on filet mignon and beer for an entire summer will do that.)

Even as someone who was familiar with the walk of shame and the art of sharting, this was a whole new level of embarrassment. I made my way through the crowds of ritzy tourists, who were staring at my stained pants while their Vineyard Vines–clad pets tried to sniff my crotch.

When we got back to the parking lot, it was time to come clean. I had to announce to all of my friends that I had peed my pants and was taking a day glo–coloured medica-tion for a UTI. Luckily, Charles's libido was not deterred by a little bladder infection and some orange pee. We laughed it off and made out. After a few days, my pee hole stopped burning and my urine went back to a normal clear colour.

What didn't go quite back to normal was my relationship with Charles. That very week, Laura's boyfriend came to visit and brought his friend, Nate. It only took me all of about five seconds to decide that he would be my next boyfriend. With the cooler weather coming in, I began to write the closing chapter on my summer love. Nate, however, would have to be continued.

LESSONS LEARNT FROM DATING A SERIES OF BOYS THAT ARE COMPLETELY WRONG FOR YOU

And boy, did we continue. Even though I was back in Florida and he was in New York, we talked all day, every day. Then I moved up to Boston for my first semester, which conveniently put me driving distance from Nate.

Do (or Don't): Discover something new about your boyfriend.

Nate and I commuted back and forth to each other for almost two years. It made me start noticing the captain/copilot dynamic, and how it correlated to the general relationship, every time I got in a car with either a boyfriend or another couple. I now believe that how a couple travels together will foreshadow the future success (or failure) of the union. And it's even worse to witness this interaction when you're the third wheel. For some reason, you automatically have to be the referee. While trying not to choose sides, it takes every bit of restraint to keep from yelling at your friend, 'You guys are horrible together! You're insecure and your loser boyfriend will never move out of his parents' house. I don't care what kind of GPS you have, it will never navigate you to success in this relationship!!!'

Now, I've been on my fair share of road trips and can tell you that, seven out of ten times, if the couple driving the car is screaming, punching or arguing about anything involving the speed, aggressiveness or safety of the driving, their relationship is probably headed to the dump. (The other three out of ten are probably masochists who get off on abuse.)

Nate and I were no different. We planned a leisurely road trip in upstate New York one gorgeous June afternoon. You should be aware by now that I'm a self-diagnosed ADHD Mexican jumping bean, so I have a bit of trouble sitting still in cars. Usually I bring a bag of toys to keep myself occupied but, on this particular day, I did not have a sudoku or a tranquilliser handy.

So I opened the glove compartment, read about the stereo in the car (still couldn't figure out how to change the clock), then smelled the paint marker that's normally used to repair the occasional scratch (like from that time I opened Nate's car door into a wall). After that, I found a lighter, lit it and squirted my perfume on it, which resulted in an impressive flame, some burnt arm hair and me being yelled at. Five minutes later, I had my socks and shoes off and was using my foot sweat to draw steamy pictures on the windshield. I got yelled at for that too. But, shockingly, none of *this* stuff spelled relationship doom.

After exhausting my search for entertainment, I finally decided to look in the centre console. Expecting to find some loose change or old 90s CDs, I was unpleasantly surprised to find a white t-shirt. Now, I'm not normally appalled at the sight of clothing, but it was really the stench that grossed me out. You see, there was poop on it.

A bit befuddled, I pulled it out and dangled it between my forefinger and thumb. After I laughed hysterically and cringed a little, I asked Nate what it was and why it was in the car. He jerked the poop shirt from my hand and shoved it back in the console. The simple explanation was that he had been working at a construction site and had to shit. Apparently, he went into the woods and used his shirt to wipe.

Now, don't get me wrong: I have 'oops-poopsed' too many times to be disgusted by or apathetic to his need to drop one. But why he kept the shirt still baffles me. I knew him well enough to know that he wasn't considering the environment by hoarding the toilet-t; he had enough one-size-too-small V-necks at home to make the cast of *Jersey Shore* jealous.

While my mind was racing through all the reasons he would hang on to such a thing, I had an epiphany. We just weren't on the same page. Although we did tend to fight in the car, it was never our stereotypical 'Honey, don't drive like an asshole, the speed limit says thirty and you're going thirty-three' banter that got to me. It was that, this time, we had literally found shit between us in the car. Not long after that, we spun across three lanes of traffic on the Massachusetts Turnpike and slammed into the guard-rail. That's when I really knew that our relationship was destined to fail. And it did fail. Multiple times.

Our next less-than-pleasant bonding experience involved me begging to be let into the bathroom while Nate was showering. As he told me to wait, I pleaded, with a tear in my eye: waiting was not an option. He had barely stepped out of the shower and twisted the knob when I busted in. I collapsed on the toilet and let out a faint battle cry, along with a liquid substance that only dried fruit could create. He screamed in horror as the steam from the shower coated his nose and tongue with my less-than-enticing bodily aroma.

Knowing that no relationship could survive what I had just done, I subconsciously began sabotaging us. I would strategically start fights so that we could go on a 'break', giving me that special grey area to make out with a different crush. And, when said crush would crush my dreams, Nate was always there to fall back on. It made me wonder: 'Why do I keep doing this to him? He is so kind and stayed with me even though I dropped a load in front of him.'

And you know what? I truly don't know why I kept doing that to him. But I did know that I simply couldn't get past the shit between us in the car. What kind of person wipes with a shirt and then keeps it in a hot car in the middle of summer? This was clearly not a man I wanted raising my kids. Could you imagine the taunts a twelve-year-old would receive at school for having a poop-smeared shirt? Poor kid would just think it was normal, 'cause Daddy does it!'

No. Poop of the Loom boy had to go. Most couples in a doomed relationship have that one glaring issue they can't get over, an issue that can only be described as unsolvable shit between the two of them. It just so happened that our shit was literal.

ADHD Break Time

Didn't that last story make you want to play sudoku?

		8			9			6
	5		1	2	6		9	
	9	2			7	3	4	
7			6			4		
	8	6				9	2	
		1			5			8
	1	5	9			7	3	
	3		4	8	1		6	
4			5			1		

In case you don't know how to play:

The objective of the game is to fill all the blank squares in a game with the correct numbers. There are three very simple constraints to follow. In a nine-by-nine square sudoku game:

Every row of nine numbers must include all digits 1 through 9 in any order.
Every column of 9 numbers must include all digits 1 through 9 in any order.
Every three-by-three subsection of the nine-by-nine square must include all digits 1 through 9.

It might also be fun to take a break and go Facebook stalk that girl you used to envy in high school. I bet she's gained three kilos, and it will make you feel amazing. (If she is still just as hot and successful, it's okay too. She's due for a fall. You rule.)

Do: Think twice before joining the Israel Defense Forces.

With the Nate break-up finally behind me, I needed to get out of town. And luckily, I had just the place to go: Israel.

The worst thing about your twenties is not being able to attend summer camp anymore. Yes, you can be a camp counsellor, but your days of getting third-degree sunburns and calluses on your hands from kayaking and basket weaving are long gone. There's no more flirtatious hand-holding in friendship circle with that super-cute boy from Philly, no more girl time with that producer's daughter who 'totally skied with Jennifer Aniston and Brad Pitt in Telluride', and you are definitely past the age of being able to sing Coven's 'One Tin Solider'[1] at the top of your lungs at any random point in the day.

On the bright side, this also means that you no longer have to worry about pouring alcohol into your ears to avoid an infection from murky lake water. And THANK GOD there are no more timed two-minute cold showers, or deer ticks to be plucked from unimaginable places on your body. But still, I often found myself longing for organised group activities. Luckily, if you're Jewish you can experience summer camp one last time.

---

1   Growing up, I spent seven summers at a camp called Eagle's Nest in the Pisgah Forest in North Carolina. Not only did they teach me how to make a fire, they also taught me all of the songs my mom probably used to get high and sing to.

Welcome to Birthright. Located in the historically rich land of Israel, Birthright is your salvation from your last year in college or your first entry-level job. It's also your time capsule back to that magical time in your life that is summer camp. Technically, Birthright is a program funded by some super-wealthy Jewish families that allows you to go and tour Israel (for free) in an effort to educate and raise awareness. But really, it's camp.

In the summer of 2007, I was ecstatic to pack my newly purchased North Face backpack and catch a cab to JFK Airport for a flight to Tel Aviv. The only person I knew joining me that session was Laura's friend Craig. He, like me, was raised Jewish and was super-interested in learning about our ancestors and, oh yeah, taking a free trip to Israel. Which, of course, we wouldn't admit to anyone else. We were there because we were God's Chosen People, duh.

Craig and I bonded on the plane by talking about my Betty Boop–themed bat mitzvah and his high-school experiences as a lifeguard for his local Jewish community centre. When we were finally loaded onto our tour bus, we were given our name tags and introduced to our chaperones and our new lifelong friends.

We got to know each other by playing icebreaker games. The first one we did was where you make three statements, two true and one false, and the group must guess the lie. One girl stated that, one, she had twelve dogs; two, she was raised Christian; and three, she had hiked Mount Everest. Of course everyone immediately knew number two was the lie. Why would a Christian end up on our Jewish rite of passage trip?

Turned out that girl did not hike Mount Everest. She was, however, a dog-hoarding Christian. WTF? She quickly explained that her grandmother was Jewish and that was why she was there.

Even though nobody said anything, we judged. It was obvious she was totally using her faded heritage for a free trip. People immediately started mentally questioning everyone else. I suddenly felt guilty that 90 per cent of the reason I was in Israel at that moment, with those people, was because it was free. It wasn't that I didn't want to be Jewish or see Israel, it was that I didn't have any money. I admitted my motives to Craig, but I didn't want anyone else to think I was a Birthright free-trip digger. I began to get increasingly paranoid that people would find out my terrible secret.

Now, I don't mean to stereotype, but I don't think I look particularly Jewish. My mom converted to Judaism, as did my dad's mom. I'm super watered down, and as blonde as the sky is blue. I was 100 per cent the blonde sheep. Another thing (besides my hair colour) that made me different from the average American Jew was my college major. I was not on track to be a lawyer, doctor or jeweller. I was a marketing major at Emerson, and casually hooking up with a Catholic guy. Thankfully, I showed off my Jew skills when I chimed in loudly with the candle-lighting prayer at Shabbat. 'That'll show them,' I thought as I *baruch ata Adonai*-ed my way into their hearts.

If you've ever been on a Birthright trip or looked at someone's Facebook album from theirs, you'll very quickly realise that everyone does the exact same things:

party cruise on the Sea of Galilee
hike to the top of Masada
camel ride
tearful tour of Yad Vashem
quiet time at the Western Wall
overnight camp in the desert
bonding time with Israeli soldiers
Shabbat dinner

My time on Birthright was the same. Except I had a challenge: proving my Jewishness.

I began this task by making Craig fall in love with me. I obviously needed a Jewish husband, and he was a total pre-med babe. Next, I made a mental note to join the Jewish college club, Hillel, when I got back to Emerson. By day three, I was going by my Hebrew name, Shulamit, and had Craig convinced we would need to own a second home in Israel.

One of the most influential things to happen to me on the trip was my time with the Israeli soldiers. As a requirement, Israelis must serve two to three years in the Israel Defense Forces (IDF). That means it's normal for nineteen-year-old girls to tote around their purses and AK-47s. I was sold. I was aware that I had no real weaponry skills, but learned I could contribute by becoming a social worker. And I would still get a super-cool gun. After a really intense seven-minute discussion about what the role involved, I arranged for my chaperone to sponsor me and let me live in his family's home in Tel Aviv.

Later that night, he announced my new life plan to the entire group. I'm not kidding. We all sat in a circle in one of the hotel's banquet rooms and my chaperone explained (in detail) my selfless choice to join the Israel Defense Forces. It suddenly became completely undeniable: I was totally the most dedicated Jew in the room. And a liar.

When I went home and broke the news to my mom that I was dropping out of school and moving to Israel to serve my country, she laughed. Loudly. She was like, 'Summer, no, that was a free trip to Israel.'

I was relieved to have my mom as an excuse to back out on my promise. It's not that I didn't really want to move to Israel and serve in the IDF, it's that I was a nineteen-year-old American who wanted adventure, but may have been a tad bit delusional. I started to feel embarrassed. My fellow Birthright travellers were all my friends on Facebook. Would they be looking for updates? Did I owe them an explanation?

It felt like that one summer at camp when I told everyone that I was an actress. When they asked me what I was in, I explained that I was in a new HBO miniseries directed by Tom Hanks. Which I was. As an extra. (It's not my fault they cut my other non-speaking scene.) I remember the intense anxiety that followed. I dreaded the next summer at camp but, it turned out, bigger things had happened for us to focus on. Like my period.

Just like the movie star lie, I decided to nervously laugh this off. I didn't come right out and make a statement, but when people would ask about my new life plan, I would blame Donna. (That's what moms are for, right?)

As the months passed and I wasn't publicly scorned for not joining the Israel Defense Forces, I started thinking. How could a two-week trip in Israel with a bunch of strangers make me want to give up my college education, friends, family and life in America? I MEAN, I PUBLICLY MADE A PROMISE TO JOIN THE ISRAELI ARMY! And then it hit me: the trip was designed that way. First, you get to form some really good friendships. You party together, go hiking together and eventually make out together. Then you get to know some Israeli soldiers who are absolutely incredible humans. And then you go and tour the Holocaust museum, where you cry and feel angry and want to do everything in your power to fight for the Jewish people. For *your* people. I can see why I wanted to move there. (I feel like a Kool-Aid joke is inappropriate here, but that's how I felt.) Everything was laid out perfectly to make you feel proud, depressed, guilty and hopeful all at once. Which is okay. Not to mention that I totally wanted to prove my Jewishness.

Long story short, I ended up finishing college and marrying a non-religious ex-Christian. And no one from my trip ever questioned my Jewishness (to my face). I still love being a Jew, and I love and support Israel, but I know that I simply don't have the chutzpah to be a soldier there. But that doesn't make me, or my future kids, any less Jewish. Which is why they deserve a free trip to Israel too, right?

> Do: Get some Boston Common sense.

As you can probably tell, Mama Donna and I are the best of friends. No matter how far apart we are, we talk every day. She's always around to offer crucial advice for whatever world-ending issue I may be having. (Typical warning from Donna: Putting Listerine on your vagina to cure a fungal infection will make you feel slightly drunk.) But she's not just great for feminine body stuff; she's also awesome when it comes to boys. Her history is chock-full of failed relationships and embarrassing moments for me to learn from. Unfortunately, it seems like I keep insisting on making my own mistakes. (See: premarital sex with losers, farting in bed and sleeping with an entire circle of friends.)

For the most part, Mama Donna accepts my outlandish ways and is eternally there for me. But she got a bit fed up with me in my college years because I was binge drinking and dating total, utter douche bags after breaking up with Nate. She spent those four years lecturing me about alcohol, condoms and pride. (I spent those four years drinking, keeping Trojan in business and misplacing my pride.) I think it's safe to say my college experience aged Donna a good fifteen years.

In my senior year, I was twenty years old and living in a studio apartment on the bottom floor of a brownstone in the Back Bay area of Boston. Donna had helped me move in and loved that I had found a 'charming, Mary Poppins–style neighbourhood'. The Back Bay is full of very affluent families, and (not to be too creepy) offers some really good people-watching at night. I loved gazing into windows and seeing how my neighbours decorated their homes. I guess you could call this furniture-watching.

But back to my place. My studio featured a mezzanine bed over my living room, which I got in and out of via a ladder. The apartment itself was actually rather shabby, and only had two temperatures: 'engine room of the *Titanic*' or 'iceberg that sank the *Titanic*'. (But isn't it just about location, location, location?)

One night, though, the air in my apartment was shockingly perfect. It was a cool September evening, and I didn't need to flick on the AC or twist the knob on my radiator. Instead, I just cracked my window to let in a light breeze. Around midnight, I closed my book (It was *Marley & Me* – THE DOG DIES?!?!?!) and tried to think of happy things, such as dogs NOT dying, when I heard, 'Summah! Summah! Open up.'

I knew exactly who this was. With an accent like that, it could only have been one of two people: Mark Wahlberg, the movie star, or Marc Finn, my Bostonian tryst. We had both ripped each other's hearts out in the previous three months, stepped all over them and agreed to see other people. But now, here he was: drunk and at my door. Of course, I let him in (I was secretly still obsessed with him) so he could sleep on my couch. As much as I would have loved to talk about 'us', I knew midnight wasn't a good time to try to convince a drunk college kid to love me. Not to mention, I had cross-country practice the next day at 6.30 a.m. We said goodnight and turned out the lights.

After waking up early and quietly gathering my stuff, I snuck out the door. I spent an hour lapping the Boston Common while my cross-country coach, John Furey, yelled out, 'Sum, pick up ya knees, this isn't a fall foliage touah!' But how could I pick up the pace? I had more important things on my mind. SUCH AS MARC FINN.

I headed home, assuming that he would be gone. Donna and I were on the phone together (with me, of course, venting about Marc) when I walked in and whispered, in a serious tone, 'Shit'. My mind was reeling: he had moved into my bed. Without another word, I hung up on Donna and put the phone on the mantle. Then I just kinda didn't notice that she started calling back, repeatedly. It's hard to blame me; the phone was on vibrate, and I was a bit preoccupied with Marc. He talked me into making him a breakfast consisting of oatmeal, fresh strawberries and kiwifruit. (I swear this kid is so manipulative, he could talk the knickers off a nun.)

Donna, on the other hand, was having a shit fit. She knew the history between this boy and me, and that he had a new girlfriend. She first imagined Marc and his jealous girlfriend lying lifeless on the floor, a heated lover's quarrel over him being at my place resulting in a murder-suicide. Obviously she didn't want blood on her daughter's hands. Then she imagined another scene, where his girlfriend was waiting to shoot me as I walked through my apartment door. A mother's fear was barrelling out of control.

After twenty manipulative minutes, Marc had finished his breakfast. We were leaning against my kitchen counter, giggling about something, when my door swung open. Laura and two cops strode in, saying that there was a report of a domestic disturbance. I explained that there was no problem, and one of the cops responded, with a straight face, 'You need to call your mother.'

Laura looked at Marc and me, pointed a finger, and simply said, 'No.' Apparently, Donna took my unresponsiveness to her call-back attempts as a matter worthy of the Boston Police Department. That's why she called Laura (knowing she had a key) and the cops. Later, Donna explained the gruesome scenes she had been envisioning, her only daughter being manhandled by some dickhead drunk college kid. And, come to think of it, my emotions *were* being manhandled by a drunk college kid.

Leave it to Donna to have those maternal instincts all the way from FLORIDA. Yes, my mom called the cops for me from over a thousand miles away. Talk about a mother–daughter ESP connection. We call ours 'Experiencing Summer's Pain'.

Don't:
Get
blindingly
drunk.

'Hi, my name is Summer and I have horrible taste in men.'

'Hi, Summer.'

Back at Emerson for my final semester of college, I was trying my very hardest to stay single and independent, for my (and Laura's) wellbeing, but I was also super freaked out about graduating and moving to Colorado for my first real job as promotions manager for a footwear company. There was only one conceivable way to deal with my stress: find my soulmate, obviously.

When Megan came over from the University of Utah to visit me, we decided to go to Daisy's, a tiny downstairs bar on Newbury Street. Always hopeful to meet a Red Sox or Patriots[2] player, I tried to frequent this place as much as possible. We began sipping on some Long Island Iced Teas, followed by a few SoCo Lime shots. (That's Southern Comfort with lime, for those of you who don't binge drink at bars.) And, as I said, I was in that weird, insecure place in my life where I was desperate for a boyfriend. I was also not seeing straight. (Maybe it was that iced tea from Long Island.) In between laughing obnoxiously and taking high-angle pictures with Megan for Facebook, I noticed a wicked hot guy. Basically, he looked like a hotter version of Ryan. I just *had* to approach him. And that is as far as my memory of that night goes.

A couple of days later, I got a phone call from a guy … a guy I met at Daisy's. He had a lovely Boston accent and called me his Southern belle. I kept trying to remember his name or face; I mean, I was basically a regular at Daisy's. I started doing a mental recap of all of the men he could have possibly been. (I used to be pretty loose with the old digits.) All I could remember was a guy who looked like my ex. Oh, or maybe it was the waiter!

My solution was to go in one night to see if there was a spark with the waiter. There wasn't. After further mental digging, I concluded that this *had* to be the high school–sweetheart doppelganger. Which was awesome, because we had a date set up for the following Thursday.

---

2   The crème de la crème of men!

All dressed up and ready to go, I kept peeking out my window to see what kind of car he would pull up in. Oh, and I should probably tell you that, at this point in my life, I was a snob. (It wasn't until I moved to Australia and had to drive a $300 1989 Corolla for two years that I realised a car is a car.) I cringed as I watched a beat-up Geo Prizm[3] pull up to the front of my building. And then my phone rang. I slowly walked down my building's front steps and sank down into the passenger seat of his car.

This date marked a momentous occasion: the first time I truly understood the meaning of 'beer goggles'. Because, through my 'sober goggles', he was much less distorted and much more rotund. His eyes were also a little bit too close together, and his hair was beyond gelled. I couldn't believe I'd set myself up on my own terrible blind date. Served me right for getting so blind drunk.

As you can imagine, the date did not go well. We went to Anna's, an awesome Italian restaurant in the North End. Dinner was great. Our chemistry was not. Let's go over the things I learned about him over pasta:

1. His name: Dillon. (Fine.)

2. His occupation: turf-keeper at the local high school. (Fine.)

3. His ex-girlfriend: life story of, and pretty much everything they ever did together. (Not fine.)

This was the first and only time that I ditched a date. It wasn't like I left him high and dry, I just insisted that I was exhausted and would walk home (the 3.4 kilometres) to my apartment. In heels. (Totally believable, right?)

After that, a year passed where I managed to not black out from drinking. I was doing adulthood proud. It wasn't until I was visiting Boston over Christmas that I found

---

3   The Wikipedia entry for the Geo Prizm says it all: 'An entry-level compact car.'

myself back at a bar with my girlfriends. That night, someone introduced me to a friend of a friend.

Boy, did I recognise his face this time. Hi, Dillon. We laughed about our date from hell and the current, more-than-awkward reunion. Then we carried on with the night. Reliving that horrible date reminded me to never allow blacked-out Summer to set me up on dates again.

Well, I must have misplaced that mental note. Not even a month later, I rekindled my relationship with Nate. This would have been fine, except that he was still a douche bag. *And* I accidentally blacked out while we were drinking together, and set myself up on a mini-date with Craig, who I ran into in the parking lot. Nate did not appreciate me making out with Craig on our date. Obviously, I denied, denied, denied (then commenced make-up sex), and continued to date Nate for a few more weeks. (I love the power of vagina.)

And then there was Jake.

Don't:
Be fooled by
a good story.

Okay, first you need to hear the love story that wasn't a love story. When I was in kindergarten, I met a boy named Jake. We became fast friends. One bumbling game of Doctor later, and our friendship blossomed into love. We would share everything, including Cheerios, Hungry Hungry

Hippos and our germs. One evening, after an incredible performance in our class play, his mom broke some not-so-good news: Jake's dad had taken a job in Pennsylvania. My love would be moving, in a matter of weeks.

The next day, during art class, we discussed our options. In the end, I realised that I was five. There was a lot on my plate, and I had my whole life ahead of me. I simply couldn't commit to such a challenging relationship. We were good together; but was that enough? No. We said our goodbyes and let each other go. If we were meant to be, we'd find our way back to each other. I kept a picture of us on my grandmother's fridge for some time but, eventually, it was taken down. Not because it was a painful memory, but because my dance recital photos were particularly phenomenal that year.

Time passed. Elementary school dissolved into awkward middle-school years. Then came high school, which brought new love and over-plucked eyebrows. It also brought an early graduation, which allowed me to forgo my last semester in order to follow my dreams to LA, remember? After giving up on that dream, I was waiting at LAX for my flight home. Sitting with my legs crossed on top of my suitcase, I was doing some in-depth people-watching. It was only broken up when my bag was kicked out from under me.

Some cute boy had accidently knocked it with his suitcase. After the obligatory 'Oh, I'm so sorry' banter, he took a seat next to me and we began chatting. When I told him that I was going to Gainesville, Florida, he started asking if I knew a whole string of people. I did know them, because he was literally listing my entire synagogue congregation. Then, LIGHT BULB. I got the feeling that this was Jake. Like, first boyfriend, love-of-my-playpen-life Jake! I asked, 'Are you Jake Stein?' He replied, 'Summer Land!'

After a few aborted attempts at getting together, he instant-messaged me out of the blue and I ended up taking a road trip with Sarah to see Jake at his college in Georgia. That weekend was magical. We laughed, played and definitely felt a spark.

But there was a catch. He was moving to South Africa, in a week, for his last semester of school. Our feelings were clearly a bit stronger this time, so we emailed each other the whole time he was there. Towards the end of my semester, he invited me to come visit. I was not willing to let any obstacles get in the way of our love again. So I set off to London to catch a flight to Cape Town, South Africa.

I am not exaggerating when I say that my week there was exactly like a romantic comedy. In between seeing penguins and petting cheetahs, we found time to let ourselves get lost on wine tours and enjoy the hot tub of the private little cottage that he had rented for us. Then we visited a township, where a friend of his showed us around and introduced us to people.

Quite a bit of our time was spent with a group who had just brewed their own beer. It was customary to sit down and pass around the beer (which was in a rusty paint bucket). When it got to me, I summoned my inner frat boy and took three gulps. Three *large* gulps. An extremely warm and flat substance, which tasted like a homeless man's urine-soaked blanket, coated my throat. I passed the can while picking some rust flakes from my teeth. When we went to leave, I told Jake that I wasn't feeling very well. He shot me a serious look and said, 'Oh my God, you actually drank it? Why didn't you just pretend? Do you know how they make that? They boil the ingredients in that fire bin over there and then leave it out for two weeks to ferment!'

FML. Now I was feeling like shit for no good reason. Why hadn't he told me that I was supposed to fake it? I was just trying to have an authentic experience and impress him. Not sure that worked. Thankfully, I didn't get sick or die. Really dodged a bullet there.

But boy did Jake impress *me*! For months, I had been talking about how badly I wanted to see lions. But Jake said that it would be hard unless we went on a safari, which we didn't have time for. On my last day, he told me we were going to a tobacco factory. I put on a fake smile and said, 'Oh how fun. You know, I have had the most incredible week so far. I'm not even mad I didn't see a lion.' Just as I finished that sentence, we pulled into a parking lot with a sign that said 'Lion Park'. I SAW LIONS!!!!!!!!!!!!!!!!!!! They were amazing.

After returning to the US for my college graduation and a mini life crisis (don't worry, we'll get back to that), I was off to Thailand for five weeks with my brother. I was truly sad to still be apart from Jake, but we were finally great at keeping in touch. In fact, on my flight out of Bangkok, he sneakily asked for my confirmation number and ended up changing my destination from Boston to Georgia, so I could visit with him and his family. It was just too perfect to be true. So much so, that it was actually not true at all.

After no more than a week in the real world, I learned that Jake was completely self-absorbed and had a severe case of ADHD. When we were together in Georgia I watched him float in and out of our conversations while simultaneously playing Snake on his Nokia phone. He moved to New York City, I moved to Denver, and we both moved on.

And that's the love story that wasn't a love story! I was truly baffled by the demise of that relationship. Not sad, just baffled. Now, I am not usually one to lament, but I had to figure out why such a good story had such a crappy ending. Let's examine some modern-day theories developed by loveless souls all around the world:

The Speed Theory

Speed refers to the movie about 'the bus that couldn't slow down'. The theory states: Relationships that start under intense circumstances never last. You can't maintain the foundations on which they were built (adrenaline and excitement). I think this theory also extends to extreme fairytale dating situations, too. With everything so perfect in our childhood relationship, Jake and I just couldn't live up to our expectations in the real world. (By 'expectations' I mean white horses, castles and happily ever afters.)

The Traveller Theory

The theory states that relationships established in La-La Land will crumble once in the real world. It's easy to fall in love while backpacking the world without a care. Of course you work well when you're in a tent; who doesn't want someone to snuggle up to when lying on a bed of rocks and roots?

I think I got caught up in the magic and the grand gestures in Africa, rather than the boy I was sharing them with. You can't blame me for not seeing the douche beyond the lion pride. But I probably should have known, since it had happened before.

Remember when I went to Israel on Birthright and fell in love with Craig? I was 100 per cent convinced that we needed to get married and make Jewish babies. Why? Because he was a cute boy from New York, and he was in Israel with me and had a familiar accent. Once back in America, I realised that he was way too emotional, which I found out when he came to visit me in Boston. I couldn't make time for him, and he felt 'abandoned'. (I was also in the weird stage where I really only liked the boys who didn't like me back. And this guy definitely liked me too much.)

You can't really blame me for not wanting to make time, though. When we slept together he used a condom that made his manhood 'less sensitive'. When we made condom-to-skin contact, I started screaming. This condom made my lady-hood burn like a bonfire. I cursed myself for having a lofted bed – you try climbing down a ladder while dealing with an allergic reaction to a premature ejaculation–preventing condom. You can see why this turned me off and made me less likely to clear my schedule; I didn't want to get burned again.

The Exception (aka The 'Charles & Camilla') Theory

The theory states that two people eventually form a relation-ship (and live happily ever after) because they attempted to put distance between themselves, but ultimately ended up closer than they could have ever imagined.

This was the one theory that really had me convinced that Jake and I were meant to be. It's the tale of a love that crosses through decades, marriages, babies and, at times, jealous ex-lovers. You believe it has prevailed because it is true, comfortable and, most of all, a long time in the making.

What the theory does NOT boil down to is this: 'Absence makes the heart grow fonder'. Charles and Camilla–type lovers are not soulmates BECAUSE of the distance between them; they are soulmates who HAPPEN TO HAVE distance between them.

I was sure that Jake and I were soulmates and that we would find each other. The fact that we kept crossing paths kept me believing in us. I thought that once the storm of obstacles cleared, we would settle down together and all would be well.

As far as I can tell, it was actually a combination of the Speed and Traveller theories that explained why Jake and I are no longer Jakummer (our cute tabloid nickname that also happens to sound like a 'safe word' for use during S&M). So if you are planning on meeting your one true love under the starry canvas of the Parisian night sky, or falling for a perfectly sculpted, bronzed Brazilian, I implore you to heed the warnings of these theories. You don't want to end up crying in the shower with wounded pride or sore lady parts. As for the Exception Theory still holding true for Jakummer in the future? Nah. Because, in the end, the Douche Bag Theory trumps everything else.

THE DOUCHE BAG THEORY

The theory states that, at first glance, your suitor appears charming, sweet and sensitive. After further scrutiny (roughly three dates), it becomes apparent that the relationship is off. While in denial, you continue to date him because, let's face it: he's good on paper. You two look flawless together. But, sooner rather than later, the relationship fails because your douche bag of a boyfriend cares more about his appearance and social perception than he does about you. He would rather kiss his boss's ass than perform cunnilingus on you. And that's a deal breaker, in my book.

Funnily enough, one of the biggest reinforcers of the Douche Bag Theory came after the release of my first stories. When they 'dropped', I basically spammed all of my Facebook friends and reminded them to download my e-book. I took into account the fact that I was Facebook friends with my rabbi, past bosses and my mom's friends (in other words, people who would probably not appreciate my off-colour approach to writing). They weren't included in the recipient list. I did NOT, however, delete any ex-boyfriends. A few months later, I received a rather douchey response from ...Well, you can guess ...

Please see below [editor's note: the following response has gone unedited to accentuate full douchebaggery]:

Hi Summer,

I assumed this message was semi propaganda for your e-book, but none the less it was nice to get a message from you. A mixture of not much down time and being NAME DELETED led to me not responding until now. Sorry bout that.

Things are going well for me, I am home from Shanghai, living in Falmouth, MA and working for the family business ... currently at NAME DELETED Marine Service in an accounting role. It's a pretty nice set up, I live a block from the beach, a block from work in the harbor. Life is good, Im getting paid well, running on the beach a lot, going in the ocean a lot. Planning some pretty epic travels for this year, China in early Dec, my Mandarin has been getting real strong lately ... life is looking like its only going to get better, no one should feel bad for me.

I had a boat this summer so speeding over to MV [Martha's Vineyard] was easy, spent lots of time on island. Tough to stay up with the social scene now that I am working M-F. Have been staying single since just before I saw you last summer and things fell through with my last girl. Have been feeling the single thing after living with someone, but thats starting to wear off. It's getting cold at night, which isn't helping. Not sure what to say about the marriage thing ... Exciting? Congratulations? Your the first ex-girlfriend I have had get married, strange. Guess there's plenty more of that to come haha. Good stuff though, I've gotten close enough in recent relationships to know if must be something fucking awesome when its all perfect.

Based on how long it took me to write you back and that your getting married I don't see us being pen-pals, but still it was good to hear from you. I hope your life rocks.

—NAME DELETED

Astounded by his Facebook message, I, of course, forwarded it to everyone I knew. The best response by far was as follows [editor's note: the following response has also gone unedited, but to accentuate full authenticity, rather than douchebaggery]:

I typed his email into Google translator and changed the setting from 'Douche' to 'English' and it came out with this:

I am bored and lonely, so when I saw your message I decided to re-creep on you. I feel that if I claim a non-descript over-active lifestyle as a justification for my radio silence you might forgive me through your natural curiosity due to my nonchalant mysteriousness.

Given I am an insanely insecure status-hungry person, I am going to have to feed you details of every inappropriately valued accolade I can attribute to my name.

Not to worry, I will also have the support of an age-old equation for picking up chicks that I read in *The Game*, which cannot fail: Cash + Crib = Chicks.

I'll let you know I am still on the market (engaged don't mean a thang), but I'll also needlessly recite an over-exaggerated hypothetical list of ex-girlfriends so I don't seem sad for this fact.

I guess in truth all three of my ex-girlfriends will find happiness without me, so I better get cracking because I am afraid of the dark. If you re-consider, please reference this email, find me and marry me instead because I'll still be here waiting ... and accounting.

—Yours forever, NAME CHANGE

Thanks, Google Translator.

A Donnalandish Thought on Dating:

Men are hunters. They love the chase. However, sometimes they need a little bait to entice them to the forest. Some men are drawn to monstrous sacks of silicone poking out from a tight top, while others love locks of hair whiter than the sand in Jamaica. Women are constantly tanning this and dyeing that in order to look more appealing and to find a mate. They usually spritz themselves with a little perfume to lure their prospects closer.

Unfortunately, all of these synthetic scents are masking our real human smells. All you need is a little vaginal moisture. Putting your pheromones right out in the open is a very effective way to attract a man. I recommend putting a tiny dab of vaginal secretions on your neck or wrists (pulse points) like perfume. I learned this (I think) from the book *The Happy Hooker* by Xaviera Hollander.

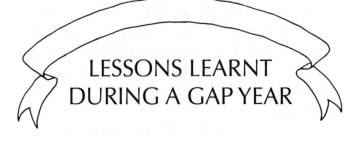

LESSONS LEARNT DURING A GAP YEAR

Graduating college was a momentous occasion in my life. Donna, Brett and I gathered in the gorgeous Cutler Majestic Theatre, and I strolled across the stage and accepted my degree with a huge grin. (I was so relieved that all the homework was over.) We had a really nice dinner out at Strega and then settled in for the night in my apartment. My mom was sleeping on my futon, but got up when she heard my muffled cries.

When she asked me what was wrong, I explained that my post-college existential crisis was beginning and I didn't know what to do next. Especially after fantasising for so long about what my life would be like after college. (It had been about eight hours since graduation and I wasn't a millionaire, so you can see why I was disappointed.)

It was pretty obvious that I was inconsolable, so Donna did what any mother would do in that situation. She climbed up my ladder to sleep in my lofted bed with me. She reminded me that I had a lot to look forward to. Such as my trip that was just around the corner!

Oh yeah, I was going to Thailand! Backpacking through Asia was a rite of passage that I could not wait to embark on. I fantasised about losing ten kilos, getting a wicked tan and spending time with monks (since I was still with Jake at the time, the monks were my best bet for safe male attention). I purchased a new North Face backpack (since the one I used on Birthright was obviously dated by months), a Nalgene[1] water bottle and a pre-distressed pair of Rainbow flip-flops. And, of course, I watched *Brokedown Palace*, which reminded me that I did not want to spend any time in a Thai prison. So drug experimentation was out.

I also watched that movie where Leonardo DiCaprio went to Thailand, found a secret island, stole his mate's girlfriend, cheated on her, copied the map to the island, caused a bunch of young tourists to die and then went crazy. (Spoiler alert: it was *The Beach*.) After thinking back on the

---

1 How Nalgene became synonymous with 'outdoorsy well-hydrated backpacker' is beyond me. I can never take a sip without spilling half of the water down my top. Plus, they aren't even that cute.

events that took place on my trek through the 'Far East', I *wish* that I had pulled a Leo.

When in Thailand, one should try to avoid being irrational and impulsive. This is especially important when it comes down to having someone pierce your skin with an ink-filled needle (which may or may not contain a communicable disease) to give you a piece of 'art' that will stay on your body forever.

But, as you already know, I have a history of disregarding the impulsive tat rule. I rarely say no, and when I *do* say it, no usually *does* mean yes. Quick recap: along with the sperm tat, my regrettable tattoo list includes a terrible tramp stamp (I should have just had 'STEREOTYPE' tattooed across my lower back[2] – it would feel more honest) and a white-ink tattoo on my wrist that says 'Alchemy'. That last one I got with Laura in 2007. (People either think we are really into medieval chemistry, or that we are finding our personal legends with help from Paulo Coelho's *The Alchemist*. I promise, it's the latter.)

My trip was derailed when, two weeks in, my friend Erica decided that she wanted to get the inside of her mouth tattooed with cheetah print[3]. The two of us went to an internet cafe to read the reviews of local tattoo parlours. I mean, it's not like we were just some stupid Americans drunkenly deciding to get inked in a Third World country, right? We were responsibly doing our research first.

The internet cafe charged fifteen cents for an hour, and you couldn't wear your shoes inside. So I removed my two-dollar knock-off Chuck Taylors and stepped into the Holy Thai Internet Palace. Shortly after sitting down in front of

---

2   My editor and I were talking about how it's interesting that sometimes the tattoo itself doesn't date, but the location can and will. Lower backs are just so 1997.

3   Why cheetah print? Because this is Erica Durgin we're talking about, aka my friend who needs an entire book to herself.

a computer, I scraped a large amount of what appeared to be pubic hair off my feet with my pant leg. After an hour of extensive research (ten minutes of googling 'tattoos in Bangkok' and fifty minutes on Facebook), we found Tattoo by Boy on Khaosan Road. Time to go!

On my way to the cafe's checkout counter, I looked down and saw a six-inch-long dead cockroach. Is it weird that having my bare feet under a computer desk with dead prehistoric insects scared me more than getting a sketchy tattoo in Thailand?

We took a 45-minute cab ride ($US5) to Khaosan Road – the gateway to Thailand! Once we arrived, we were saddened to learn that Boy did not do oral tattoos. But I was not about to leave empty-handed. I had been meaning to get another tattoo anyway. I felt incomplete with only the two horrible ones that I've mentioned numerous times and that decent 'Alchemy' one. This was my chance to get another wrist tattoo and redeem myself completely.

Approximately seven minutes later, I decided to get the Dutch word 'Buitenverwachting' in white ink. Why, you ask? I had just visited South Africa (with Jake) and went to a vineyard with the same name. It translates to 'Beyond Expectations'. Almost as quickly as I had decided to get my newest soon-to-be-embarrassing permanent body art, the experience was over. I was bandaged up and sent on my way. The next morning, I woke up with my new tattoo and a revelation. Little did I know, white ink can oxidise and BECOME GREEN. So now half of my tat was the colour of a shot of wheatgrass. My wrist looked like it was rotting. It would have been perfect for a 'Thriller' revival performance.

Since I am used to ugly tattoos, I didn't freak out. Instead, I calmly went back to Boy and asked him to go back over it in white. In the process, Boy made the 'c' into an 'o', which only added insult to injury. Plus, his redo didn't even help the colour. Now, my tattoo was a half-green, misspelled Dutch word. I knew that the only thing that was going to cheer me up was a shot of snake's blood and a Thai ping-pong show. Turned out, girls shooting balls and bananas out of their vaginas did *not* make me a happier person. The anger caused by that tattoo was not going to go away easily.

Throughout my trip, I stayed consistent by doing the opposite of what I set out to do. I had allowed a dread-locked Thai man to tattoo my wrist with white ink, and I gained three kilos. (Damn Singha beers.) Once I was back on American soil, I got tested for hepatitis and made an appointment to get my tattoo removed. (I didn't have hepatitis, but a faint outline of the tat still lingers.)

Now that you've relived this experience with me, I hope we've all learned some valuable lessons. The main one being, I should never ever get another tattoo. Actually, I think a few years in a Thai prison would have been less embarrassing and more enjoyable than my years of awkward tat explanations and laser removal treatments.

> Don't:
> Get a nine-
> to-five job.

Once I got back from Thailand, I moved to Colorado to start a job as the community manager for a footwear company. I basically helped establish their online presence, arranged wear-testing and organised celebrity endorsements. Seeing as I was living in the tiny town of Parker and *not* Vail or Breckenridge (beautiful ski resort towns), I was mildly depressed by my surroundings. Rural Colorado isn't exactly what this self-proclaimed 'city girl with expensive vacation taste' needed. My new world consisted of strips malls, tumbleweeds and a Carl's Jr[4]. Aside from one rich neighbourhood, the majority of the homes there looked like they housed meth labs.

About three months in to the job I discovered two important things about myself. One, I hated working nine-to-five, and two, I definitely did not know what I wanted to be when I grew up. I decided to escape to Park City, Utah for the weekend to visit Megan and her family. (They had relocated there from Florida a few years earlier.) I had been twenty-one for a little over a week and needed a proper celebration. (Since it was a work night when I turned the big 2-1, I stayed in and watched *The Notebook*. Alone. In my unfurnished apartment.)

I set off on the eight-hour journey to Utah, only stopping for beef jerky, gas and gum. Other than that, I was singing every lyric to Heart's 'What About Love' and (I confess) anything by Eve 6[5].

Megan and I decided to get some drinks with friends at Kristauf's, a cute martini bar at the bottom of Main Street. Two martinis and two Sidecars later, we ventured to Star Bar at the top of Main Street. After dancing our hearts out to Lady Gaga, we piled into a taxi (responsible) and went home to Megan's parents' house. While a bunch of people played in the hot tub, Megan and I changed into pyjamas and headed to the kitchen. There, we stood over the sink and crammed handfuls of Smartfood White Cheddar

---

4   Which served as a constant reminder that no matter how many Carl's Jr hamburgers I consumed in my time, I was nowhere closer to looking like Paris Hilton.

5   Actually, not guilty about this.

Popcorn into our mouths. The only interruption of our binge came in the form of a South African guy who needed to go home. (Well, he wanted to stay. But we needed him to go home so we could enjoy our unattractive ritual of stuffing ourselves with food and talking about what kind of moms we would become.) I hadn't had a drink in a few hours and thought that I had to be at, or below, the legal limit of .08, so I offered to give him a ride.

We piled into the car and blared some Murray Head on the stereo. Megan, South African Boy and I all sang, in unison, 'One night in Bangkok and the world's your oyster!' Apparently, my in-car dance moves must have caused me to swerve (a tiny bit) because, before I knew it, my rear-view mirror was filled with blue and red flashing lights. It was Labor Day weekend, so I should have remembered that there would be a massive infestation of police officers.

I turned down the music and pulled over to what was obviously a DUI checkpoint. There were already three other cars lined up, along with various inebriated humans trying to walk in straight lines and touch their noses with their index fingers. An officer approached my window and asked for my licence and registration. My licence was in Megan's purse, and when she handed it to me I dropped it in between the seat and centre console. Fail. I actually had to get out of the car and move my seat back to reach it. With the electric seat-adjusting motor moving at a glacial pace, the cop had just enough time to suspect that I was almost as wasted as Mel Gibson in a pool of vodka.

Mr Officer asked if I had been drinking. Scared shitless, I said, 'Yes, I had a few drinks, hours ago.' This was true. It was also true that I did not have a firm grasp on my blood-alcohol content. I was sure it would be at .08, but wanted to play it safe. When the cop went to his patrol car to run my licence, I quickly asked Megan to grab some pennies from the cup holder. I shoved them into my mouth and sucked on them, while Megan looked at me like I was straight out of *One Flew Over the Cuckoo's Nest*. I started explaining (with a mouthful of change) that I had remembered a bit of wisdom from an old Boston friend. He once told me (in his wicked-thick Boston accent), 'Summah, I heard that if ya evah get breathalised, to suck on pennies because it will lowah ya BAC scoah.' At the time, I thought it was hilarious. In the present, I was desperately hoping it was true. If not, I was probably just going to get trichomoniasis for nothing.

As the cop was walking back to my car, I was scared he would see me raise my hands to my mouth so, in a para-noid move, I spit the pennies out into my lap. Reality set in when he asked me to complete a field sobriety test. I got out of the car (thankfully the officer did not notice the pile of pennies fall off my lap) and walked over. While taking the test, I thought I was passing with flying colours. I walked a straight line, touched my nose and balanced on one leg. Apparently that was not good enough. My eyes were red and my tongue was chalky; that meant I had to blow. Deep breath in ... long exhale. I silently prayed, '.08, .08, .08[6].' Nope. My BAC was a whopping .117. That's when I was told, 'You have the right to remain silent. Anything you say or do may be held against you in a court of law ... yadda yadda yadda.' I put my hands behind my back, and on went the cuffs. (Exciting!)

While sitting in the back of the police car, I spotted Megan, who was on the phone with her parents (eeeeeek). The only thing she could possibly have been saying was, 'Summer is in the back of a cop car and being arrested for a DUI.' Low moment.

---

6   I don't know how people drink anything and drive in Australia. My BAC reaches .05 if I accidently squirt out too much hand sanitiser.

Mr Officer drove me to the county jail and made me stand in the parking lot for an extended period of time. And it was cold. Like, Utah-mountains cold. When I asked if I could go inside or get back in the car while he finished his paperwork, he replied with, 'You want to talk about extreme weather?! Try spending a winter in Afghanistan!' (Which was kind of beside the point, I thought.)

Way to make me feel like a weakling (and the most worthless human ever). In an effort to be nice and make conversation, I asked if he happened to catch a Jessica Simpson concert while he was serving overseas. No, he did not.

Left alone with only my thoughts while Mr Officer did paperwork (or played Farmville on his phone, I'm not too sure which), I really started to think about my current predicament. Part of me was completely devastated and felt like a low-life scumbag. The other part of me felt like I was in a movie. (Please note: under no circumstance do I condone drinking and driving. But I *do* think getting cuffed is really exciting. All of the greats have been arrested: Bill Gates, Martha Stewart, Kid Rock, Lil Wayne and Lindsay Lohan … just to name a few.)

Donna always told me that if I was going to get arrested, I should do it before I turned eighteen. When the cops came to break up a house party during my high-school years, I got off scot-free. I guess it was just my time.

When I was finally allowed inside, I learned that the booking process was just like it is in the movies … but about six hours longer. Cops are really good at (as Donna would say) lollygagging around. They had me remove all of my jewellery, and report my tattoos. (I only reported the wrist one. Now my FBI record says that I have an 'arm tat'. Badass. I know I should have listed them all, but seriously, try explaining the sperm tat to a cop.)

Then it was time to line up for my mug shot. After asking, repeatedly, for a mirror and some MAC foundation, I was informed that I wasn't allowed to freshen up. So I ran my fingers through my hair and used some spit to wipe any mascara residue from under my eyes.

As a former model (by 'model', I mean I once got to sit in a Limited Too store window in a mall for a couple hours), I decided to give my best bitch glare. You don't want to seem pompous by smiling in your mug shot, but you also want to avoid looking sad and sorry. So I settled on the 'don't take no shit from nobody' straight face. (Later, when Megan sent me my picture from the Summit County website, I was so proud.) The only other awkward thing that happened during my jail photo shoot was when they told me to turn left. I turned left, but then looked back over my shoulder. The police officer angrily told me, 'This isn't Glamour Shots. Look left.' Jeez, sorry (not sorry) for vogueing.

I'm not sure if you're aware, but when you get to make a phone call in jail, it's from a payphone. And it's a collect call. Seeing as it was 2008, and no one I knew had a home telephone number, I got special permission to use the station's non-payphone. I dialled Megan's cell (the Donna call would have to wait), and she told me NOT to call a bail bondsman (there went plan A). Instead, she and her mom, Sally, would be there to get me out as soon as possible.

Once situated behind bars, I met my super-sweet cellmate, who looked just like Molly Ringwald. (Well, a mascara-stained Molly Ringwald who had just been arrested for a DUI.) After I made her laugh with a 'We got no food! We're in jail! Our pets' heads are falling off!' *Dumb and Dumber* joke, she let me share her blanket.

Around 6 a.m., I was finally summoned by an officer and told that I had been bailed out. Molly Ringwald look-alike and I said our goodbyes, and I exited the holding cell.

I don't know if it was the exhaustion, the alcohol or the sheer embarrassment, but I was suddenly a wreck. I burst through the doors and into Megan and Sally's arms, in tears. In retrospect, I realise that there are a number of reasons for this unexpected eruption of emotion:

1. I had just been arrested for the first time and spent a night in jail.

2. I realised I had a second family who loved me enough to bail me out of jail even though I drove (with their daughter) while under the influence.

3. I let society down by driving drunk.

When I went to thank Sally for the bail, she laughed and said she'd used her Amex, which got great points so it was really a win for both of us: I got out of jail, and she got free airfare.

When we got home I went straight to bed, and woke up around 9 a.m. (Nothing like getting a solid three hours in dreamland before you remember that you're a failure.) Megan's parents were legends, though. Not only did they forgive me for being a completely irresponsible idiot and endangering their kin, but they also recommended a phenomenal lawyer. Within the hour, I was in touch with him and scheduled for court.

The next thing I had to do: face Donna. Now, the thing about my mom is that the fear of disappointing her is much greater than the fear of any kind of punishment. I called and broke the news, but she didn't lecture. She offered love. When I asked why she was being so kind, Donna explained that, back when she had a fake-out heart attack (it was just gas) and hadn't told me she was in the hospital, it was because she didn't want a lecture from me about her weight and fitness. Therefore, since the tables were turned, she decided not to lecture me about my enthusiasm for alcohol or lack of a brain. God, I love Donna.

This experience really taught me a lot. After twelve weeks of a court-ordered DUI Information class, fifty hours of community service, a $2000 fine and a $5000 lawyer bill, I learned that getting arrested is cool, but not *that* cool. If you want to experience jail, don't drink and drive. It's dangerous, embarrassing and, all in all, a pretty reckless thing to do. So, if you absolutely *have* to find out what it's like in the joint, may I suggest public urination and/or intoxication? Even if you don't get charged, you're gonna have a good time.

Do:
Cherish your friendships.

When Megan's family moved to Utah full-time in 2005, I started making a trip every March for spring skiing[7]. Her family always made me feel so welcome. It's not that Donna didn't give me all of her love and more, it's just that Megan's is the perfect all-American family. They wear matching pyjamas at Christmas, have an extremely organised pantry

---

7   My skiing experiences before that had been a little horrific. If you ask Donna, she'll tell you that there's nothing more terrifying than driving through snow and looking into the rear-view mirror to see your son's eyes glaring at you through a black fleece mask. Actually, it's slightly more terrifying when he grabs the front passenger seatbelt from behind and pulls down with all of his force, pinning your daughter against the seat. As he tries to slice through her torso, your daughter musters a blood-curdling scream. It echoes through the vehicle as she spits out her partially chewed processed chicken all over the dashboard.

and love family portraits. It's always so much fun to play house with them.

On all of my many visits (pre-arrest), we would beg Megan's dad, Roger, to hire an instructor for us so that we could 'get the hang of skiing again'. And, of course, we would request a male in his early twenties. It eventually became obvious to Roger that the only thing we really needed to 'get the hang of' was flirting.

It was always a futile effort, though, seeing as 90 per cent of the twenty-something instructors were Mormon and already married. Luckily, Megan and I quickly learned that the other 10 per cent were Australian, English, European or South African. And it was even better when we discovered that we didn't need to pay for a lesson to get their attention.

Two weeks before Thanksgiving 2008, Megan was out at a bar when she noticed a guy playing on his BlackBerry. Since Megan is Megan, she ran over and asked him to become BBM (BlackBerry Messenger) buddies with her. His name was Paul and he was Australian. His friend, Aaron, was English. They got to chatting with Megan and soon realised they were living in the house directly across the street from her.

I came over to Megan's for Thanksgiving. Since we were both very single, Megan and I thought bringing over some leftovers was the perfect opportunity to welcome these new guys to the neighbourhood (and, hopefully, our lives). We quickly rushed through dinner, loaded up some plates with stuffing, turkey and cranberry sauce, and trekked across the snow-covered yard to meet the guys. We knocked on their door and, within an instant, Paul caught my eye. I decided to use the whole 'flirt with your stare' method, which seemed to work. The next night, we all went out to Star Bar, and Paul and I kissed right in the middle of the dance floor. Success!

In January 2009, just after my run-in with the law, I ended up moving to Park City full-time. I wasn't ready to have a grown-up job, and luckily Megan and I discovered a whole new world of seasonal work and ski bums. And Paul.

That winter, I underwent a transformation. You see, I'm what the ski community would call a 'gaper': someone who skis the groomed runs, wears Obermeyer ski gear and puts the bar down on the chairlift. Horrified that my new friends didn't love my new $350 North Face ski jacket, I didn't dare tell them how I used to dress on the slopes in high school. But don't worry, I *will* tell you.

When I was fifteen, I borrowed ski clothes from Ryan's mom, Yvonne. And by 'ski clothes', I mean some 1986-Aspen-coke-dealer ski clothes. I loved them. One day, I chose to wear her tight black jumpsuit (including stirrups, so my boots really stood out) that had a bright yellow top with faux fur around the collar. The outfit was really brought together by cinching my waist with a black belt with a silver buckle. Since I'm Summer Land and really obsessed with all things Britney Spears, I also put my hair in high pigtails. Then I hit the slopes feeling like the sexiest little snow bunny on the west side of the Mississippi River.

Brett and his friends decided to spend some time hitting rails and jumps, while I opted to go get my downhill ski on, alone. I ended up sharing a chairlift up to the peak with a nice man. As we casually talked weather and slope conditions, I just couldn't get over how cool I must have looked in my gear. When I went to exit the chair, I angled my skis to do a sharp left turn. (It's always crucial to make a smooth exit.) Unfortunately, my impossibly tight ski clothes somehow snagged on the chair, not letting me go (it was like something straight out of a *Final Destination* movie). The chair jerked my body to the left and turned 180 degrees, almost beginning its descent back down the mountain. Thankfully my new friend notified the lift crew, and they stopped the machine just in time. After they got me loose I surveyed the new holes in Yvonne's pants and in my ego, and thanked them for their help.

I *so* didn't want another experience like that to happen in front of my new friends. If there's one thing I learned from my time in Park City it's that, in order to fit in at a ski town, you need to be steezy. To better explain this, I feel that we should turn to the Urban Dictionary.

> steezy – (adjective)
>
> A snowboarder term that combines the words 'style' and 'ease' to create the act of doing a trick with style and ease to make it done with super steez. Whether it be because of his/her tricks, gangster apparel, or whatevs.
>
> Example: 'Yo man, you see that gangster killin it? He's got some hella steez[8].'

Now that we're on the same page, we can conclude that locals are steezy and vacationers are gapers. To honour this, there is an actual Gaper Day in Park City, during which the locals dress up in old-school one-piece ski suits. (It looks like the whole mountain raided Yvonne's closet, which, I admit, I find awesome in a totally unironic sense.)

Unwilling to confess that I was once a full-fledged gaper, I quickly adopted the steezy style. I traded in my fitted clothes for baggy pants, tall t's (which can be found at Wal-Mart in size 2XL) and beanies. I would wear my ski goggles at all times in an effort to work on my goggle tan. (This is particularly crucial if you want to be considered a

---

8   So apparently it can also be used as a noun.

local. The only thing more important than your goggle tan is how many days you have skied by the end of the season. Seriously. The 'number of days skied' tally is considered even more important than the 'number of girls slayed' tally in Park City.) With a firm grasp on how to be a ski bum, I gave up groomed runs and started venturing to the park, to try to hit jumps, boxes and rails. Key word being *try*.

Do: Make out with men with accents – especially Australian ones.

One 'blue bird' day, there wasn't a cloud in the sky so Megan and I were on the slopes with Paul the Aussie and Aaron the Pommie. (I was fully decked out in my new gear, which, in my personal opinion, did not do anything for my figure, but whatevs. At least it was hiding the seven kilos I had put on from drinking PBR tall boys[9] every day. And, more importantly, it allowed me to fit in.) Anyway, I was really trying to impress Paul and make him love me, so I decided that I was going to go over a jump (for the first time ever). After watching other humans fly through the air and land as gracefully as Shaun White at the X Games, I had decided that it would be easy. So I pushed off and began my descent to the medium-sized jump. That was when I heard Paul yell, 'SLOW DOWN!'

---

9   The budget beer of choice for most skiers, boarders, hipsters and backpackers.

No way was I going to slow down! I wanted to show off and catch some 'mad air'.

Well, I definitely did catch some mad air. Not only did I clear the jump, I made it all the way to the next jump: quite the overshoot. Unfortunately, I didn't land as smoothly as I had intended. With poles, skis and my body flailing, I managed to flip around and land directly on my face. Hard. Like, rockem-sockem-punch-to-the-face hard. And, just like in a cartoon, little birds and stars circled around my head.

Megan and Aaron came running to my side, followed closely by Ski Patrol. Megan wiped the snot and blood from my nose as the medical team checked for any major spinal injuries. They then asked me to speak. All I was thinking about was my face. Had I lost any teeth? Was my hairline still intact? What about my nose??? So I looked up and asked, 'Am I still pretty?' (Which I think is a fairly valid fear. When I was younger and would go on trips with my friends' families, Donna would write a medical consent form that included a paragraph granting permission for any cosmetic procedures in case my face or body was mangled. So you can see where my concern stemmed from.)

Once they'd confirmed that, despite the temporary presence of two black eyes and a nose swollen up to 'Marcia Brady after taking a football to the face' proportions, I still had my good looks, and I'd confirmed that I knew the day of the week and who Barack Obama was, I was helped down the mountain. I kept looking around for Paul. Why hadn't he come to my aid? We had been consistently hooking up for like a solid month.

When we caught up later, he said that he didn't want me to be embarrassed, so he rode away. Well, now I was even *more* embarrassed. How can you *not* be embarrassed in oversize ski clothes with a very bruised nose and two black eyes?

But I couldn't really confront Paul about not being more sympathetic and attentive. We weren't technically 'boyfriend and girlfriend'. Yes, we continued to go out every weekend and woke up most mornings together, but every now and then he would do something that would make me hate him. Yeah, 'hate' is a strong word, but you'd hate Paul too if you brought a friend to one of his house parties and he took her to bed instead of you. (No, she is not my friend anymore.)

I was crushed when this happened, but decided to act like a Stepford wife and be overly understanding when Megan and I ran into Paul at the Corner Store (a ski-in, ski-out bar) a few days after his 'indiscretion'. I took the moment to bat my eyelashes and said, 'Oh, Paul, we're not even dating. It's fine. I mean, you're a complete asshole and I never want to hook up with you again, but that doesn't mean we can't be friends.' The look of guilt on Paul's face was apparent; obviously, the kid felt bad. He probably thought that he had completely destroyed my world (which he had, but I wasn't about to let him know that). I continued my aloof monologue about how we were going out that night and he should come.

As most normal (completely crazy) girls would do, I spent the night trying to make him jealous. I flirted with boys in front of him and even found one to kiss. But no one compared to Paul. I really think that there was something going on with our pheromones, because my body just kept telling me to mate with him.

A few days later, one of our friends got a hotel room at the Marriott on Main Street. We all decided to have a little hotel party and play in the pool. Paul and I withdrew to the pool so that I could stand on his shoulders and do backflips into the deep end.

When I swam back after landing one of the most perfect backflips ever, Paul asked, 'So does this mean we're going out?'

OMFG PAUL JUST ASKED ME OUT.

I smiled and tried to sound cute when I said, 'Uhhh, I don't know.'

'Because I only have the clothes I came in.'

OMFG HE WAS TALKING ABOUT GOING OUT TO A BAR AFTER.

'Oh yeah, I mean, if we do, I'm sure we can go home and change.'

AWKWARD.

Even though he hadn't asked me out for real, it was obvious that there was something more this time. That night, Paul and I acted as couple-y as couples get. He bought my drinks, watched my purse when I danced on stage with Megan and even kissed me on the dance floor in a non–*Jersey Shore*–face sucking way. It was special.

At the end of the night, Megan and I went home and Paul and Aaron stumbled across the street to their place. While lying in bed with Megan, I couldn't stop talking about Paul. He was going back to Australia at the end of the season and I didn't know what to do. I wanted to keep our adventure going, but didn't really know how to commit to a boy who was committed to being a notorious man-slut with a love of travel. There was no way I was going to be able to make him a) love me, b) commit, or c) let me join him on his travels.

Trying to sell my new plan to Megan in exchange for her best-friend support, I said, 'I think I want to go to Australia on a Working Holiday Visa and travel around. I don't know where I'm supposed to live or who I'm supposed to be. I kind of want to keep travelling.'

'Liar. You are so totally in love with Paul.'

Clearly she saw right through me. I tried a new angle: 'Come with me.'

'No thanks,' Megan said breezily as she examined her cuticles. 'I don't really have the desire to live out of a suitcase and drink cheap beer. You know me. I like brie, resorts and wine cellars.'

'If round-trip flights are under $800, I'm going to book it.' I got out Megan's laptop and went to Qantas.com. I typed in LAX to SYD. Flights were $790.00. Totally a sign that I just *had* to go.

'I'm booking it. Are you sure you won't come?'

'Yes, I have a full-time job, Summer. And it's too far to only go for a week. You should go, but promise me that you guys will come back next season.'

'Promise.'

'Smell my bellybutton.'

'What? No!'

Megan fingered her belly hole and then shoved her hand right in my face. We laughed (loudly) and rolled off the bed. Megan then straddled me and held my hands down while screaming, 'Smell it!!!!!!!!!'

Just then Megan's mom opened the door to tell us to keep it down. I tried to apologise, but Megan's body weight was crushing my solar plexus.

'I don't even want to know. Goodnight, girls.'

We spent the next hour giggling about smelly bellybuttons and boys.

LESSONS LEARNT WHILE BACKPACKING AUSTRALIA

Saying goodbye to Megan at the end of the season was hard. We decided to spend every waking moment of our last week together. Literally. We woke up, ate breakfast (turkey sausage and eggs), played tennis, had lunch at one of our favourite restaurants, Squatters, and then played in her hot tub. On our last night, we chose to have a spa night instead of going out. Megan's shower doubled as a steam room, so we undressed and both got in to start sweating out our toxins. There really wasn't much space for two people, but we did our best to squeeze in together. We were having a pleasant time exfoliating each other's backs when Megan let out a blood-curdling scream. Her right calf (she has enormous, perfectly toned calves) had pushed up against the metal mouth where the steam came out. She immediately opened the shower door and screamed for Sally to come and help. I told Megan to lie down on the towel on the floor so that I could really see the damage.

'Oh, Megan, it's the exact shape of the steamer,' I said in an awed tone. (It really was perfect.)

Megan wailed, 'HOLY MOTHER OF GOD, MY LEG IS ON FIRE.'

When Sally ran in, she didn't notice the burn because we were still completely naked. 'Why are you girls always naked?'

'MOM! It hurts so bad please make it stop!!!'

'Summer, run and get the first-aid kit. But maybe clothe yourself first.'

I wrapped a towel around myself and then ran to retrieve the kit and came back as quickly as possible. Sally treated the burn and wrapped Megan's leg.

'Are they going to have to amputate it, Mom?'

'No, sweetie. You'll be just fine. Maybe you two should consider showering separately from now on.'

Megan and I both said at the exact same time, 'Never.'

With Megan's injured leg wrapped in gauze, we made our way to the airport the next day. It was time for me to go and find my personal legend[1] in Australia. And time for my reunion with Paul.

When I got to Los Angeles to board my international flight, I felt super-cool because I was wearing my North Face backpacker's backpack. (The one from Thailand!) I mean, I looked like I might as well have been trekking the entire Appalachian Trail. Alone. With only a guidebook for figuring out what plants and berries were edible. In a word, I was a complete badass. (Or is that two words? Oh well.)

As I stood in line waiting to check in, I got a preview of what was in store for me when two tanned men with bleached-blond locks walked up behind me, smelling of salt water. We accidentally[2] made eye contact. The cuter boy started talking in an intoxicating Australian accent.

---

1   Paulo Coelho told me I'd find it one day. Do: Read *The Alchemist*.
2   You know this wasn't an accident. I'm a shameless flirt and you know how I feel about eye contact.

'How ya goin'?'

My mind tried to translate the words coming out of his mouth, but obviously I was hitting a cultural-differences wall.

I happily chirped back, 'To Australia!'

'No, how yaaaaa goin'?'

'Uh, Qantas. Flight QF11.' Sheesh, this guy was pushy.

'No, I mean, how are you?'

'Ooooohhhhhh. I'm fine, thanks!'

I was quite surprised that I didn't know the whole 'how ya goin'' thing, seeing as I had been talking to Paul and other Aussies the whole season before. Suddenly, I was nervous about not being able to communicate once I got there.

After the first hour of the flight, which I spent thinking about language, I spent the other fourteen hours thinking about Paul, our relationship and what I was going to do in Australia. He and Aaron already had jobs at Perisher, a ski resort in Jindabyne. I was really over being ridiculously cold all of the time, so I had plans to meet up with my college friend Emily in Perth. (I would have felt like a stalker if I'd tried to work at the same place as Paul; plus I'd have to live at least thirty minutes away. I didn't want to seem desperate!)

Joining Emily was the perfect plan. Emily is the best girl's girl. She approaches major life issues (waxing fails, boy problems and girl fights) exactly the same way as she approaches her web design business: with great skill, expertise and powerful execution techniques. She was raised in Boston and can do a wicked good Boston accent, but her Midwestern accent should not be forgotten. It's incredible.

Emily had already been in Australia for six months, and had eating cans of tuna and rolling her own cigarettes down pat. If I was going to make it as a backpacker and not a 'flashpacker', I definitely needed her guidance. The two of us, along with fifteen other travellers, bought five four-wheel drives and set out on the rocky trail from Perth to Darwin.

It was a four-month journey that did me proud. We slept outdoors the entire time, discovering the meaning of life around camp fires beneath a canopy of shooting stars and the famous Southern Cross constellation. A German guy would play Oasis's 'Wonderwall' on his guitar every night. (If I had a dime for every German backpacker playing 'Wonderwall' on a guitar somewhere in the world at this very moment ...)

Many fascinating things happened to me when I was living in Australia (some a bit more agonising than others) and, for the most part, I left feeling like a brand-new person, with a brand-new asshole. Literally, if you recall my cliff-jumping adventure.

Do:
Practise
queefing.

Recently I was lying in bed when I decided to suck air into my vagina and push it out. The sound it created startled my cat and got me thinking about the wonderful world of vaginal flatulence.

Let's go back to the first time this happened to me. The monumental year was 1997. I was a normal ten-year-old, on my L-shaped couch, watching a block of cartoons including

Rugrats, *Doug* and *Rocko's Modern Life*. In between inhaling Totino's Pizza Rolls (fresh from the freezer section) and Hi-C Ecto Cooler juice boxes, I found myself on my back with my legs above my head. While flailing around, I accidently tensed my muscles, causing air to rush into my vagina.

Well, what goes in must come out. So I pushed and made the most awe-inspiring sound ever. I had discovered the queef (aka pussy fart, aka fanny fart, aka nani poot, aka one of my future party tricks for years to come). Within an hour, young Summer could suck and release on command. I even experimented with the wide variety of sounds my new musical instrument could create by holding my hands over my opening as I pushed.

Fast-forward five more hours, and I was in the bathtub, learning that I could suck in water, too. Yup, I was hooked. As someone who lives for bathroom humour, the idea of a fart sound with no smell was an extraordinary discovery. Of course, I immediately had to teach this skill to all of my friends.

The genital concerto tutorial went something like this: 'It is definitely easiest to achieve when you have your legs above your head. However, with proper exercise, it is possible to strengthen your muscles and achieve the fanny fart on your back, or while standing up. This may take extra concentration and designated practice time.'

Sure, I recall lying on my stomach with my butt in the air when I was even younger and accidently sucking air into my rear. But boys could also do that, so it wasn't too exciting. There was also the very grave possibility that I would probably poop my pants. Not for me. Instead, my ability to nani poot separated me from nearly half the population. Not only is the vagina a holy grail in itself, but now mine was also a musical instrument.

For years, my little trick stayed between my girlfriends and me. It was not until I started having sex that I learned that you could queef accidentally. This is always an awkward moment between couples (ranking right above the chest fart). Yes, the only time that farting isn't so funny is when you are physically joined with someone. (Unless you're into that sort of thing.)

Usually, I save my queef-on-command trick for friends or social gatherings. However, I would like to introduce a new use for the vagina's vocal chords. This one came about in Australia.

Due to the exorbitant amount of time we spent sleeping in shared tents, everyone became extremely close. During the trip, one of the girls lost her father due to a very aggressive form of cancer. We were all together when we found out, and decided to gather the girls in one of our SUVs to console her. (There also may or may not have been a little herbal refreshment being passed around.)

For the record, I tend to get nervous in serious situations and find myself trying to be Captain Comic Relief. So, naturally, I brought up queefs. The mere mention of them evoked so much laughter and curiosity that, within minutes, they had me on my back, sucking in air, over and over again. That's right, I was fully consoling a crying girl with my musical vagina. I had heard of music therapy and art therapy, but the healing power of fanny farts was something new.

Of course, with any new and unconventional form of medicine comes criticism. One girl in particular didn't receive my unorthodox comic relief very well. In fact, she was horribly disgusted and offended. Now, normally I would be more understanding of her reaction, but this girl ripped normal farts on a regular basis. I know it's hard to remain ladylike in the outback (especially when you make unwanted eye contact with a dingo, spider, crocodile and/or kangaroo every time you relieve yourself), but this girl could gross me out. Almost every day, a warm and heavy stench would add even more humidity to the air in the car. Once you ruled out a dead animal, you would see her toothy smile in the rear-view mirror. She had no shame. You think you know someone, and then they fart in a car full of people. Then again, you may also think you know someone, and then they turn their vagina into a whoopee cushion for attention. To each their own. But at least I was helping someone in need.

Not to be too egocentric, but I like to think that my queefs have brought joy to the world. Laura and I have spent many nights reminiscing and giggling about all the hours we spent creating a duet with our lady parts. And I know Aaron enjoyed the five consecutive toots that my vagina made when Paul and I tried to 'cuddle' in the bed next to him (quietly).

The person who I have probably shared the most queef-joy with has been my Aussie friend Jodie. She, too, has mastered the art of fanny farting on command. Unfortunately, she discovered her vaginal abilities during sex with her boyfriend. Embarrassed, she tried to cough to mask the sound. While using her lips to help mimic the noise her vagina had just made, she sounded like something along the lines of, 'ahempffff, excuse me, blipffffbap.' I find this incredibly endearing and, even more so, entertaining.

We ended up having a contest (in front of all of our friends) to see who could make the loudest queef. After two rounds of 'pffffffff' and 'flllrrrraaaaaaa', we were pretty much neck and neck. I was also getting pretty weak down there. As I sucked in my last puff of air, I pushed my hands into my crotch and magnified the sound as I pushed with every single muscle in my vagina. Hands down, I came out as the winner. But in the interest of sportsmanship, I feel like I should admit that I just got lucky. So let's consider this my official challenge to a rematch: Best two out of three, Jodes?

Don't:
Be bummed if you're mistaken for a stripper.

In the sixth grade, Cherish and I took a break from studying kabbalah and decided it would be fun to put on fifteen layers of clothing and do a striptease (on our teacher's desk) in front of our friends. The plan was to get all the way down to our bikinis, and then go to swim time. Our prepubescent bodies bumped and grinded to K-Ci & JoJo as we yelled, 'Put the money in the bucket' and sipped our sugary SunnyDs like glasses of Cristal.

Apparently, some of the little kids in school must have used their fake IDs to get into the big kids' classroom (I'm so proud of them). I started hearing that the third-graders' parents were less than thrilled when their eight-year-olds came home expressing their aspirations to become exotic dancers, 'just like Summer and Cherish', when they grew up. After that, we were no longer allowed to be inside the school building unsupervised. And thus, my budding stripper career came to an end before it even got the chance to blossom.

My next encounter with the legendary world of exotic dancers (aside from the Thai Sexual Magic Show), surprisingly, did not occur until ten years later. After Emily and I repaired my butthole after my infamous cliff jump and finished our road trip, we stopped in Darwin for six weeks to earn some money. (I had spent all my cash on the plane ticket, meat pies and cans of flavoured tuna.) Darwin, famous for having no rules, its mammoth-sized crocodiles and being filled with generally shady characters, was also a haven for us backpackers.

After sleeping in a tent for 14 weeks, and then being homeless for two nights in a town park, I jumped at the opportunity to share an apartment with six fishermen (who I had just met). Granted, this sounds like it was probably not the safest or brightest thing to do. But, after nearly four months of sleeping on rocks and being mauled by insects that I hadn't even known existed, I would have been willing to snuggle up to an echidna if it promised me food and shelter.

My new roommates decided to take me to a quaint little bar for Stripper Night. The only girl in our group, I catapulted myself into a pick-up truck full of seamen to see the future Jenna Jamesons of Australia. Having never been to a strip club, I was incredibly excited. Since I have never been able to play 'correctly' with poles in any playground (I'm accident-prone, extremely unco and ridiculously inappropriate), I couldn't wait to see a pole being properly used and in its natural habitat. I yearned for these exotically beautiful women to show me their night moves while they tried to 'lose their awkward teenage blues' (thank you, Mr Bob Seger).

When we arrived, however, it felt more like I was 'back in America, y'all'. As in, the southern part of America. Yeah. A fog machine and George Michael's 'Careless Whisper' set the whole mood. The bar was filled with cigarette smoke and cans of the outback's finest alcoholic beverages.

I had been expecting lasers and advanced lighting, coupled with the kind of techno that makes you instinctively eat drugs and dance with glowsticks. My hope was to take a seat at a stage that doubled as the bar, so I could sip a Dirty Martini while easily reaching my dollar bills into fluorescent-yellow G-strings.

But no. None of that happened. And the 'stripper stage' was the greatest disappointment of all. It was basically a card table, with a roped-off area in front. You actually had to go under the rope to get to the bathroom door. Never one to judge too soon, I ordered some food and waited patiently to see what amateur adult entertainment would take place.

It was after I'd consumed the greasiest, soggiest fish and chips on the planet that the night took a drastic turn for the worse. Feeling alarmingly queasy, I began getting food sweats as the first stripper took the stage. She must have been a very dirty girl, because she proceeded to take a bath. Kind of. She was squirting herself with soap and putting poor Rubber Ducky in unspeakable places. During her performance, I really couldn't focus on anything other than the fact that she was so willing to apply soap to her vaginal area, with almost no water! If I had attempted such a feat, I would have had thrush and a raging bladder infection within minutes.

In between thoughts of burning pee holes and rubber ducky porn, my nausea was increasing by the second. That bar meal was not sitting right. Luckily, there was a break after stripper number one. (I'm assuming it was because she needed some time to rinse off all the soap, take a cranberry pill and retrieve Rubber Ducky from the depths of her rectum.) Hunched over in pain, I crawled under the rope, raced across the stage and threw my face into a toilet. Then I proceeded to make dinosaur noises for five minutes.

After swearing off fish and chips for the rest of my life, I looked in the mirror, wiped the vomit from my lips and flushed my face with refreshing brownish bathroom water. Finally, I re-braided my pigtails and made sure that my jean skirt was straight. As soon as I was somewhat composed, I walked back out. Lucky for me, I knew I hadn't missed anything because they were announcing the next stripper. Unlucky for me, the bathroom door opened directly onto the stage area. Everyone started cheering, thinking that I was the next stripper. Despite immediately questioning my outfit choice (was it passable stripper wear???), I realised that this was my moment. It was my chance to smile seductively and flawlessly perform the moves that I had been practising since I was five.

Instead, I froze. The room went silent; the lights illuminated my body and blinded me from being able to see anyone in the audience. Before I even had time to bust a move, I licked my lip and tasted the partially digested fish chunks that were still crusted to my face. I panicked and quickly stumbled off stage, mumbling, 'I'm not the stripper! I'm not the stripper!'

To top it off, my awkward exit caused me to trip while trying to get back under the rope. Everyone began booing me! Apparently, Vomit Girl isn't as appealing as Soapy Vagina Girl. I totally blew it.

Afterwards, I took a seat at my table and was bombarded with Australian accents and semi-flattering comments.

Aussie Boy # 1: 'Oy! You should've got ya tits out, hey?!'

Aussie Boy #2: 'Yeah! You totally could've gotten on the pole!'

Aussie Boy #3: 'I'd root you over those birds up there!'

Aussie Boy #1: 'Yeah, that schoolgirl shit is old.'

Aussie Boy #2: 'You're hot because you have an American accent and most of the pornos I watch have American girls.'

Aussie Boy #3: 'You should do porn.'

I started feeling like someone who had just failed her final exam at stripper school. But then, I thought to myself, maybe it just wasn't my time. I deserved better than a card table for my debut as a bona fide stripper. I deserved *Playboy*. So I held my head high, knowing that my moment would come. In the meantime, I am proud to say, it was the only time in my adult life that I have been mistaken for a stripper (thus far). That fact, I am sure, is one that makes my mother proud.

Do:
Wear a bra.

One of the main reasons I'm afraid to be a stripper is that I don't feel comfortable with my body. I have really small breasts. And it's been an issue for YEARS. Ever since I was little, I've had some serious boob envy. I am not exaggerating by saying that I was completely obsessed with the idea of cavernous cleavage.

At age ten, I began reading about my breasticles (aka breast buds, aka the hard nubs on the chest that develop before actual boobs). I spent my nights clenching my chest muscles, with my hands clasped, while singing the old, 'We must! We must! We must increase our bust!' chant. Then I started to make sure that I was always sleeping on my back … to allow for growth.

About a year later, I was confident that my boobs were going to sprout any day. I would constantly fondle the little ant bites in search of any sign of progress. Finally, one day, I noticed something extraordinary: perfect, tender, round balls that would be the foundation of my soon-to-be sumptuous breasts. I instantly invited all of my friends and family to feel my development. After about three months of somewhat dubious little-kid boob handling, my breast buds disappeared. I shit you not. And I swear on Donna's life, it's because I touched them too much.

Accepting the fact that I was not going to be able to facilitate the growth of massive jugs on my own, I commissioned the help of several chest-enhancers. These items included, but were not limited to, the miracle bra, water balloons, regular balloons (the tied end makes a great faux nipple), toilet paper, gel bras and socks. Oh, and, lest we forget, my water bra. (Side note: I got the sweetest message from my friend's mom, Kathy, recently. She was reminiscing about the time I showed her what a water bra was. I was ten. She was forty-seven.)

All of these things were intended to bring my body to fruition. About ten years (and ten awkward toilet paper exposures) later, I came to the realisation that I simply had tiny tits. It was time to embrace them. No boobs? NO BRA!

The thing about having small tits is that it does not necessarily mean you have small nipples. In fact, I have a little bit of an above-average areola region. If you drew a circle around my chest/stomach, you might confuse it for a pepperoni pizza. This made going braless a little socially unacceptable. In my teens, I once decided to wear a very seductive shirt, which was basically a bit of cloth strategically placed over my nipples. That night, I was getting my dance on at a nightclub when I noticed a slight breeze from a massive fan pointed at the dance floor. Of course, I was pretty engulfed in my own thoughts about how hot I probably looked with the wind blowing through my hair. But then a stranger came up to me and said, 'Uh, your nipple is showing.' Yes, that fan had blown my 'shirt' clear off my right boob. This was when I learned two important lessons: one, fashion tape is a great invention, and two, I should definitely start using it.

Aside from always being the braless girl, I usually existed okay in society. It was not until my time as a bartender in Darwin (the hottest and most humid place on the planet) that I had some issues. I had a perpetual sweatstache and once even shit my pants at work because I drank too much bitters. (But that's another story.)

Working as an outdoor cocktail waitress for a month and a half was a terrific job while I tried to save money and kill time until I met up with Paul in Sydney. It was also great because I had to wear black, but did not have to wear a bra. I carefully chose a nice spandex tank top that worked perfectly with my little boobs. (PS, the walk-in fridge was a bonus when I needed hard nipples for those extra-rambunctious tables.)

All was calm on the braless front for a while, but then we got a new manager, Jason. Why Jason had a big issue with my small titties is beyond me. But for some reason, he decided to inform me of a new rule: when I was behind the bar, I needed to wear a bra. Stunned and embarrassed, I agreed to do so and walked away. Ten minutes later, I overheard him gossiping in the kitchen about me; he was going on about how he had to speak to me because I NEVER wore a bra and how ridiculous it was. I confronted Jason about his unacceptable managerial behaviour and then took my braless self to the bathroom to cry. I mean, imagine everyone talking about your boobs after you'd been completely braless in a walk-in fridge! Suddenly, my freedom from brassieres did not feel like a win.

When I explained my ordeal to a table of my regulars (fishermen), they laughed and told me that my nipples were the only reason they even came to the bar. That made me feel a little better. Later on, my most amazing manager ever (a beautiful Dutch girl named Fleur, who looked like Cate Blanchett) came up to me and said, 'I heard some people are being wankers to you. Well, I think you have cute, perky little breasts and you don't have to wear a bra if you don't want to!'

Boom. I didn't. Fast-forward to one week later. I was working the Melbourne Cup event at the bar and decided to be extra conscientious about my obnoxious chest real estate. So I made the effort of putting on a bra. I waltzed up to a table of important people, confidently carrying a tray of freshly filled champagne flutes. They were my beautiful (yet intimidating) Dutch manager, the general manager (a man) and the owner (another man). After having a pleasant conversation, I turned to leave, and Fleur whispered that my bra was allowing everyone to see both of my nipples. I awkwardly turned to walk away and, as a result, flipped the tray into my chest. The remaining champagne spilled down my body, and seven crystal glasses shattered at the feet of my superiors. Of course, all of them graciously made a pretend gesture to try to help. I scampered off to get a broom and dustpan, while cursing myself for not having bought a new bra since eighth grade. The one I was wearing was an underwire one from Express that did absolutely nothing to cover my woman parts. It basically just pushed my shirt out, allowing the world to see my pink stamps. This marked the beginning of my nipple exposures.

I know what you're thinking. With so many boob issues, why not just go the plastic surgery route? I could at least get them big enough to fit in an A-cup. Well, when I was twelve, Lauren's dad, Eric, made a bet with me that I would have breast implants by the time I was twenty-one. If I didn't, I would get $100. As a twelve-year-old, a hundred bucks seemed like an enormous sum of money. So I had it ingrained in my head that a boob job was out. On 21 August 2008 I received a cheque for $100 dollars and a card from Eric reading, 'A bet I am happy to pay up on! Let's just hope it's not a down payment.'

I feel like getting plastic surgery now would leave me with this weird, underlying guilt about letting down my best friend's dad. Weird, I know. So I've decided to carry on with my miniature mammaries. They aren't always easy to conceal, but a lady's gotta do what a lady's gotta do.

Don't: YOU EVER WALK HOME ALONE AT NIGHT. (This is your Summer speaking!)

Before I left Darwin I found myself walking down the street after attending 'Tits Out Tuesday' at a local nightclub. And, FYI, I did not have my tits out. (Well, not intentionally.) The night had been fun, but I could not consume another sambuca shot, and I had seen far too many G-strings and fake boobies. Although I thoroughly enjoy watching people on ecstasy lick and try to eat the air, I'd had enough. It was time to venture home to my refrigerator.

Stumbling down the street in my heels, I looked like a dinosaur: you know, that knee-bent, ass-out walk that only a prehistoric creature could pull off. Obviously, someone saw my weakened state and decided to attack.

This man, sporting wire-rimmed glasses, had clearly escaped the grasp of *To Catch a Predator's* Chris Hanson and found himself crossing my path. He was Australian, probably in his late forties, and was the essence of all things wrong. He acted very timid and asked everything in a breathy, creepy voice. It felt like when someone lurks over your shoulder and exhales heavily, leaving condensation on your skin. At first he seemed harmless, but I think my judgement was impaired. The standard 'Hey gorgeous, how was your night?' line began one of the most ridiculous five minutes of my life. Let's put this conversation into script form, shall we?

EXT. Dark and desolate street in between the city centre and the waterfront – night

Summer: (slurring) My night was fine. Just a bit hungry.

Creep of the Century: Are you American?

Summer: Haha, yeah. Am I that obvious?

CotC: You're that beautiful. What's your name? What are you doing in Australia?

Summer: I'm Summer. I am doing a working holiday, just relaxing, living the dream and backpacking. What do you do?

CotC: I'm a fisherman.

Summer: OMG! I live with a bunch of fisherman! Do you know Anthony?? What about Steve? How about Adam????

(I play Six Degrees of Separation with everyone.)

CotC: No. I don't, but it gets really lonely out there, hey? I only get to come to the mainland for about a week at a time. Six weeks at sea can make you kind of crazy. Makes you forget what the touch of a woman feels like.

Summer: (cringes) Yeah, that sucks. I think my roommates get pretty lonely too.

CotC: Let me take a picture of your nani.

(No, he didn't say nani, but I don't really like the word he said. It's gross.)

Summer: What????? NO.

CotC: Come on. Let me have a picture of it, so I can look at you while I'm at sea.

Summer: No, that's gross. No way.

CotC: Give me your underwear.

(DEAD SERIOUS. His tone changed from creepy to threatening.)

Summer: Please, no, I am so close to home. Let me just go.

CotC: I bet they're wet. Let me have them.

It was at this point that I thought it was best not to argue with the creepy man who wanted my undies. I slid them down and prayed that I had sharted in them while I was dancing earlier. (It would have been at least a minor win for me.) He took them and hurried off to the waterfront.

Then I ran the remaining 60 metres home. It wasn't until I was at the stairs of my building that I lost it. I had been so violated, it caused me to vomit all of my fear and sambuca onto the steps. Somehow I made it up the eight floors to my apartment and blacked out on my mattress.

The next morning, I woke up in a haze. My dress was on, but with no underwear. WTF? I knew this wasn't like the time I had taken off my panties to hang them in a tree. Suddenly, it all hit me. Flashback: sambuca, creepy fisherman, glasses, underwear, vomit.

I called Paul and bawled my eyes out. He consoled me and reassured me that I would be safe in his arms in no time. Emily was away on a weekend trip and was horrified when she learned what had happened. (She was especially horrified that I let her go first when we both said we had bad news. Hers was a flat tyre. I totally won.) I took a couple of extra hours to bathe and lick my wounds, and then hung my head in shame as I walked into work.

I mentioned the incident to everyone the moment I arrived. And naturally, everyone was horrified. One girl even told me a horror story about the same thing happening to her friend in Canada. Only, when she refused the man, he'd raped her.

We all agreed that I should never walk anywhere alone again, because I am too naive and stupid. It was also decided that I had to file a police report. (That was an interesting call: 'Hi, I'd like to file a police report ... I was walking home around midnight last night when this creepy man demanded to photograph me where I pee. Then he stole my underwear because they might have secretions on them.')

Later that evening, I told my mugging story to two fishermen who were sitting in my section at work. I gave them the play-by-play; they gave me their sympathy and money for new underwear. They also asked me what the guy looked like and said that the two of them would keep their eyes open for 'the sick bastard'.

About five months later, when I was back in America, Anthony, a roommate from my time in Darwin, called to tell me that he had run into two old friends. He hadn't seen them in years, so they all went out for drinks to catch up. His buddies started telling him this crazy story about some American chick who had gotten her knickers mugged from her. Later on, they had found the guy and kicked his ass! Anthony started dying laughing and told them that the American chick had been his roommate. (See? It *is* a small world! And *this* is why I always play Six Degrees of Separation!)

Ladies, I know that when we get drunk and tired all we want is some hot fries and a bed. But please don't ever walk home alone. You may think, 'It can't happen to *me*.' And then, next thing you know, some creepy man is trying to steal your underwear while you're stumbling home. On that night, I realised I am not invincible. No one is.

With so many creepy men out in the world, I realised even more how special Paul was. I had been in Australia for nearly six months and, while we hadn't been in the same place for much of it, we had been acting exactly like a couple. We talked twice a day, and when we were together we forked AND spooned, held hands and debated the meaning of life until the sun rose.

Don't: Sleep with Paul on the first date. He doesn't like that.

Emily and I left Darwin to meet Paul and Aaron in Sydney for a two-month road trip up the east coast. As we were heading back down, around week six, we stopped off at the Arts Factory in Byron Bay for a few days. The Arts Factory is an amazing camp site/hostel/hotel that is the perfect backdrop for serious life talks among backpackers. And lucky for me, I was about to get serious with Paul. Things had been going so smoothly with us, but we had yet to have the 'relationship talk'. You know, the one where you agree to start introducing each other as your boyfriend/girlfriend.

Nervous about what he'd say, I finally got the courage to ask Paul about our future one morning at breakfast.

'Listen, we're having fun,' Paul said, trying to keep it light. 'Why do we need a title? Let's just keep going how we're going.'

Fair enough. But I knew I needed to be honest with Paul. 'I can't do it like that. I can't be in limbo. Why won't you just commit?'

'Honestly?' Paul inhaled and then exhaled slowly. 'I don't see myself marrying you. You slept with me the second time I ever met you.'

I immediately got defensive. 'Paul, that is such a double standard. You are the biggest man-whore in both hemispheres. I slept with you so quickly because I was just looking for a fling. I wasn't expecting to fall in love with you. It just happened. You were Australian. You had an accent. What do you expect from us American girls?'

'I'm sorry, but I just can't.'

I stared at him from across the table while he avoided eye contact at all cost by vacantly gazing at his empty plate.

'You're pathetic,' I spat. 'I can't believe you'd let some stupid thing like that get in the way of what we could be. Love is not planned. Love is inconvenient. You can't plan everything.'

'I just want to keep travelling. I don't want a girlfriend right now.'

'Then why do you treat me like one?'

'I don't know. Why can't you just relax and go with the flow?'

There was absolutely no way I could go with the flow. I had watched way too many romantic comedies with happy endings to expect anything less for myself. 'I'm almost positive you've never seen *When Harry Met Sally*, but when Harry realises that he loves Sally he says, "When you find the person you want to spend the rest of your life with, you want the rest of your life to start right now."'

Paul said nothing.

His lack of words felt like a punch in the stomach. I knew that my only option now, to salvage my heart and what was left of my self-respect, was to get away from him.

'I'm staying here. You and Aaron should go on to Sydney without me. Emily and I are going to hang around Byron Bay. I can't keep going on with you.'

Thank God Emily was travelling with us. I needed her so much, because what Paul did next was completely earth-shattering.

He left. I know I told him to, but I didn't mean it! I mean, I wanted to mean it. But come on, I was so in love!

I watched him walk away from our camp site. I kept staring even when I couldn't see him anymore. Then I turned around, grateful to see Emily standing nearby. I walked over, wrapped my arms around her and cried. I felt like I had just been in a car accident. I tried to keep my head up and be strong and optimistic, but my world felt like it had just been shat on.

Emily was on my team and supported my decision to go on a Paul detox; she had witnessed him messing with my emotions too many times. (Little did she know, I was just telling myself I didn't need him.) The next day, we decided to get a sixpack of Coopers Sparkling Ale and head to the beach. On our way, we walked through town so that we could see if any restaurants were hiring; not only was I now single from my non-relationship, I was also jobless and broke.

I had two options: get a job and stay put in Byron Bay for a few months, or go home. What I really wanted to do was go back to Park City in three weeks when the ski season started, but Paul would be there and I didn't want to face him. Emily and I laid our towels down on the sand and took in the view of the lighthouse. No matter how hard I tried, I could not smile.

Emily, always the optimist, laughed. 'If the ocean and that view can't make you happy, I'm not sure anything will.'

After a bit of thinking, I told Emily that I wanted to go back to Park City. I was so homesick and so very tired. If I had to bathe in a public shower one more time, my feet would probably cut themselves off. I'd had athlete's foot and thrush for what felt like an eternity. I just wanted to go back to America and buy premade food in the grocery store; I wanted to live in a land where buffalo sauce and blue-cheese dressing was readily available. Fuck, I just wanted a normal doctor! The gyno I went to in Darwin didn't even give me a robe to wear; she just had me lift my skirt and pull my undies to the side to put a speculum in.

And, above all, I needed Donna.

Emily accepted that I was not strong enough to go through another six months of living in a tent. She told me that she was sad to see me go, but understood.

Next, I had to call Paul. I needed to let him know that I was going back to Park City, but needed to not know him. I grabbed my cell phone and told Emily I'd be right back. I walked down the beach a bit and took a seat on a bench, slowly dialling his number (which of course I knew by heart).

Commence the Closure Phone Call. When he answered, I told him that I had decided to go back to Park City for the season. Not for him, but because I missed America and I missed Megan and I wanted to ski again.

I told him that I needed to not be around him. I couldn't be his friend. I couldn't kiss him. I couldn't see him. I asked him to please not acknowledge me, for my own sake. I may have slept with him straight off the bat, but I was still a catch. I needed to check my pride and move on. If he couldn't get over how we got together, then that was his problem.

What he said next completely changed my world. He giddily pleaded that he didn't want that. He wanted to be my boyfriend. He explained that when he left, he almost cried. He would have if Aaron hadn't been in the car. He asked me to come to Sydney the next day so that we could spend our last few weeks together in Australia before it was time to go back to Park City.

I was stunned! 'Are you really serious?'

'Yes.'

I hung up and realised that I was smiling. I walked back over to Emily.

'So, how'd he take it? Did you get closure?'

'I'm going back to Sydney tomorrow and we're going to America and we're boyfriend and girlfriend!'

Emily rolled her eyes. 'So much for standing your ground.'

Of course Emily was sceptical. But I was too homesick and in love to listen or stick around. I arranged a share ride with a nice girl through our hostel and took the ten-hour journey to Sydney the next day. The trip felt like it took an eternity because the girl pulled over at every rest stop to smoke a cigarette. (Plus, she had a massive mole with exactly six hairs coming out of it on her left cheek that I couldn't stop staring at.)

Moles and tobacco aside, we made it to Sydney. Paul met me at the girl's house. When I got in the car he hugged me and then handed me a letter.

To My Dearest Summer,

Just a small card to say thank you for chasing me around the world. Every second you're away from me, I think about you and miss you so much. I promise the tides will turn and I'll be the one chasing you when you need to be on the other side of the world. I love your company so much and I appreciate you far more than you think. From this day forward, I promise that I'll never not be by your side for any long period of time. I'm so excited to continue my adventure with you. xoxox

From Your Lover, Paul

Turns out, Paul is a man of his word. From that day forward, he has been 100 per cent committed, loving, doting, funny and absolutely incredible. My flight back to the US was a few weeks earlier than Paul's (plus he had planned a boys' trip to Thailand), so I ended up going back to Florida and spending time with Donna (my other number one.)

Reuniting with Donna was almost as amazing as the love of my life professing his love for me. We chatted about life, went to yoga and caught up on all of our favourite sushi restaurants.

I also had the tedious task of getting all of my US affairs in order. Dentist. Car payments. Gyno.

Do: Live in a country with socialised medicine.

Sometimes I feel like I have an undiagnosed case of hypo-chondria. I always seem to conclude, after an hour of research on WebMD, that I have a combination of chlamydia, gonorrhea and syphilis from kissing a boy. Then I decide that I've thrown my life away and definitely have AIDS. (Clearly the movie *Philadelphia* strongly affected me.)

These STI freak-outs usually go something like this: I call my doctor's office and ask to be tested for everything. The conversation goes something like this:

'Do you have any symptoms?'

'No, I don't have symptoms.'

'Did you use a condom?'

'No, we didn't have sex.'

'Okay, then why do you want to be tested?'

'Because we made out and I touched his penis with my hand …'

(Uncomfortable silence.) 'And?'

'Well, can't I get something from skin-to-skin contact?'

'No.'

'Well, can you test me anyway?'

'Yes. For $500.'

Yup, I think it's safe to conclude that I am a full-blown hypochondriac. So, naturally, when I came home from Australia I decided I'd need a thorough gynaecological exam; it would be wise to get tested for all possible venereal diseases. (I was *sure* I had something this time, due to the amount of time I had gone without showering, not to mention the three days spent in Broome, sleeping behind a bush with a bag of wine for a pillow.) Of course, medical tests suddenly become much more difficult when you realise that you have to get them done *without* health insurance.

There's a good explanation for why I was living unprotected. I had let my insurance lapse when I was in Australia, and now I would be uncovered for a month before it kicked in again. Shit. I prayed not to break any bones or develop a malignant brain tumour in the meantime. But, being the neurotic chick that I am, I still desperately wanted to have that womanly exam. Immediately. And specifically, I wanted it to be in my hometown. I was moving to Utah in three weeks, and I didn't want to have to deal with any weird girl issues there. (Best to have your mama around for vagina stuff.)

With no health insurance, I didn't have much luck getting an appointment with my usual doctor. Since the cost for all the tests would be enormous, she told me I was better off going to the county clinic. (Or maybe she was just scared off from the time that I barged into her office with a *Cosmo* and told her that, according to the article I'd just read, I definitely had trichomoniasis. She told me that I had thrush and no STIs. Then she mentioned that I should calm down.)

Unable to relax without having my exam, I drove to the wrong side of the tracks, parked my car and walked through the automatic doors of the Alachua County Health Department. After taking a seat, I spent the next twenty minutes reading all of the posters, signs and pamphlets in the waiting room … in Spanish. I finally got called up to the window. Then came a series of questions:

- # What is your annual income? 'Uhhh, I get an allowance.'
- # What is the size of your house? 'I don't own a house.'
- # Do you own a car? 'I leased it. WORST decision ever.'
- # Do you have air conditioning? 'Yes. We are in Florida.'
- # Do you own a microwave? 'Yeah, how do you think I eat?'
- # Do you own a toaster? 'No, I use my microwave.'

These were just a few of the questions meant to determine what I would be paying that day. Since I was just visiting my mom for a week, I was technically an unemployed squatter without a toaster to my name; I wondered what kind of discount that would get me. With all this info written down, they finally led me through to the next part of my adventure.

Sure, Waiting Room #1 made me feel like a spoiled little rich girl who was experiencing life below the poverty line for the first time ever. But I was in for an even ruder awakening when I was told to take a seat in Waiting Room #2. The woman next to me had some rather tattered-looking hair extensions and was compulsively rocking back and forth. All the while, she was talking out loud to no one in particular. She eventually screamed at the nurse to get her some red Gatorade. Naturally, I decided this would be a good time to get to know her. I love red Gatorade, so we had that in common.

She explained that she had been waiting for hours and that the nurses sucked at their jobs because they hadn't brought her any 'goddamn red Gatorade yet'. She also told me that the devil had put the HIV in her body because she was a sinner, but it was okay because she had been going to church recently. This seemed like a good time to NOT mention that I was Jewish and that there was probably no red Gatorade in her near future.

As I sat in the waiting room, surrounded by more Spanish-language posters and Alachua County's poorest citizens, I grew a little worried. Now, I don't *usually* discriminate when it comes to who looks at my vagina, but this place was a little frightening. Thankfully, a twenty-something blonde girl with a bouncy ponytail came in and called my name. I wished my new waiting-room friend well on her quest for red Gatorade and followed Blondie back to the exam room. She asked me questions about my medical history; we chatted about which high schools we had attended and discovered some mutual friends. I loved her. Relieved and blinded by our bonding, I hadn't even realised that she was only a nurse. So you can imagine my dismay when she said that the doctor would be in shortly to perform the exam. My only hope was that another woman would come in to do the dirty on me. (I have a little bit of anxiety when it comes to male doctors.)

I got undressed, put on that robe that opens in the back and sat on the paper-covered exam table. Trying anything to distract my worried mind, I resorted to counting the goosebumps on my right thigh. (Why is it always minus twenty degrees in doctors' offices? At least it's one time that I don't have to be self-conscious about my massive nipples; they always shrivel to the size of five-cent pieces in those places.)

Finally came the knock on the door, and in walked the most ginormous African American gentleman that I have ever seen. He literally had to duck under the doorframe to enter the room. In an alarmingly deep voice, he introduced himself and said that Blondie would stay in the room for the exam. On one hand, that made me feel more comfortable. But on the other hand, I thought, 'Great. Not only do I have to get finger-banged by Shaq's doppelganger, but now one of my peers, who shares mutual friends with me, is going to witness it.'

Dr Shaq began by checking my breasts for any lumps. All clear. Time to move down south. Now, lying on a table with your feet in stirrups is hard enough as it is. But then you have to factor in the doctor pointing a hot lamp at your lady hole while grasping a plastic speculum to open you up for inspection. Super-uncomfortable. I have spent many exams nearly backflipping off the table while moving away from the doctor. Of course, as usual, after inching backwards, I was asked to scoot down (in other words, I had to put my vagina in the man's face).

My body temperature was rising uncontrollably, so it was time to shut my eyes and escape into my mind. There was a bit of an issue getting that started because, after looking at my vagina, the doctor asked the nurse to get a smaller speculum. (Awkward.) With the new, smaller device inside, he began to feel around my feminine parts. Eyes still closed, I tried to imagine I was lying on a beach but the pressure on my insides rendered me unable to find a happy place. I could only envision images of his hand bursting through my belly, fingers flailing, in a scene reminiscent of *Alien*. Approximately thirty-five seconds later, with my stomach miraculously intact, this new man-friend pulled his hand (which could be mistaken for an elephant foot) out and told me that everything looked fine. Then he casually mentioned that I had a bit of razor burn on my bikini line. I think that last comment was a little below the belt.

Feeling a bit violated, I got dressed and went to check out. On the way to the desk, I did a quick recap of what had just happened: my waiting-room friend had told me that the devil had put HIV in her; my pap smear had been administered by the biggest man in the world (with hands to match); and said man also told me that I needed to work on my bikini line. Yup, that's all in order.

As the receptionist totalled the tests and factored in my financial situation, I stood and tried to tally the final cost in my head. Assuming it would be around $250 for the most horrific experience of my life, I made a mental note of which bank account to use. (Since I was broke, I was doing a bit of juggling.) That was when I heard, 'That will be $12.74.'

I'm sorry, what????? Apparently, if you don't have health insurance, the sliding pay scale can slide all the way down to everything being basically free. On the downside, you may have to pay a little extra in terms of loss of personal pride and getting fisted by a man four times your size (which, depending on what you're into, could be a bonus).

Because of all this, I decided to wait six extra months and get an appointment with a female gynaecologist for the next time. Her office was on the top floor of a private hospital and was outfitted with chilled water and an array of lovely reading materials. Once in the exam room, I was told to go behind the curtain, take my pants off and place my feet in the stirrups on the table. After dropping trou, I looked around for a sheet to cover my lower region with. Usually they give you a gown or something, right? Nope, not this doctor. I heard her typing on her laptop as I searched madly for any kind of covering. Well, there was a mat-type thing on the table where I was to sit. So, with no other option, I decided to drape it over my body. When the doctor pulled the curtain back she quickly said, 'Ohhhh, that goes under you, not on top. For hygiene reasons.' She got me to lift my bottom and slid the mat under me, just like she was diapering a baby. I was mortified.

During the entire pap smear process, I am positive she was preoccupied with thoughts of sterilising her table. As if that wasn't enough, at the end of the appointment I mentioned an unfiltered thought: 'My mom once tried putting Listerine on her hoo-ha. Instead of nixing her itch, she got a buzz. Must have been something about the thin labial skin.'

The amount of awkward silence that filled the room made me wish I was back at the county clinic. I did my best to avoid eye contact with the doctor when she walked me to the checkout counter. What I couldn't avoid was my $390 bill. I'd take my massive man for $12.74 over that place any day.

Do: Write love letters.

With my clean bill of vaginal health, I was ready to take Park City by storm. During our second ski season there, Paul and I were officially in all sorts of 'you're my soulmate' shit. He and I were both utterly infatuated with each other. Don't get me wrong, we'd argue, as couples do, but for the most part we just couldn't wait to spend time with each other every day. Since we were on opposite schedules, we liked to leave little notes.

Dear Lover,

Sorry, I mean Summer. Please don't be upset, I hate to see you like that. The girl I'm in love with always smiles and laughs with me. Don't worry about those silly things you brought up earlier. You got $1000 today and all of those financial worries have gone away. And also keep in mind that you're probably chopping into the hottest bloke in Park City right now. Well, you will be on Saturday night.

Love, P. (Your future husband)

Can you believe that letter came from the same guy who said that he didn't respect me because I slept with him on our second date? Not only did we say 'I love you', we talked about the future all the time. By the end of the ski season we were kind of over being poor and living off the land. (By 'land' I mean 'PBR tall boys and curry'.)

We decided it was time to get grown-up jobs. (EEEEEEK!) The only dilemma was that he was an Aussie and I was a Sepo. (Summer's Aussie Slang Lesson: 'Septic Tank'. 'Tank' rhymes with 'Yank'; 'Yank' as in 'Yankee', as in 'American'. 'Sepo' is short for 'Septic', therefore 'Sepo' means 'American'.)

Seeing as it was 2010 and there were still no jobs in America, it really only made sense for both of us to move to Australia. Paul had to go back to Australia and work another season at Perisher to support himself, so I hung out with Donna for five months back in Gainesville while waiting for my visa to be processed.

Dear Summer,

Although we are going our own ways now, I assure you it won't be forever. It will probably feel like a long time, but you just need to have as much fun as possible, because time flies when you're having fun. The more fun you have, the less time it'll be until you get to see me next.

It is going to be so weird not having you be my shadow 24/7. I'm going to be so lost. I love having you hang off of me at all times. I want to take full advantage of our time together. I have never felt more in love in my entire life. You make me laugh every time I'm with you. (Not at you, but with you.) You're not only funny, but outstandingly good-looking. You're practically perfect in every way.

If you ever get sad, please read this letter and remember that there is a very high chance that I'll be thinking of you. (About 99.9%.) The other 0.1% will be me thinking of how I'm going to fix a machine or something like that. You're always on my mind and this time away is killing me. Thank you so much for teaching me so many things. You've made me such a better person. You might not think that you have but I promise you have. I love you more than life itself and can't wait to spend the rest of my life with you.

Love, Paul
xoxo

And of course, I would respond in my own special way:

Boyfriend,

Love you, I do. Make life with you, I want. Happy Birthday, I wish! [Yoda speak.]

I hope you have heaps of fun on your birthday. I am devo that I am not with you to get maggot. I'd like nothing more than to eat drugs and dance at Glass House in Wollongong with you. I can't believe what a hot bloke I get to chop into. I can't wait until we have little anklebiters running around. I hope you're ready to see your Sepo Cheese and Kisses when you get to God's other country.

I love you so much and hate that we're apart. We should look into surgery to become conjoined twins. I'd like that.

Your shadow, Summer

Don't:
Partake in
karaoke.

Being back in Gainesville was okay. I liked spending time with Donna and loved that I got to reconnect with Hillary, a super-duper cute girl from high school. She's blonde, bubbly and looks amazing in pastels. What's even better is that she has this sharp wit and somewhat surprising bathroom humour that I can't get enough of. Even though we were busy going to kickboxing religiously and enjoying beer-funnelling activities on the weekends, I also tried to visit Laura in Boston and on Martha's Vineyard as much as possible. I knew that Australia is far away. Like, time-travelling far. So it was very important for me to catch up with all of my sisters from other misters.

After a quick week on Martha's Vineyard babysitting Laura's big sister Krista's kids, I wanted an awesome night out with friends. Since it was Friday we settled on The

Wharf. I proceeded to get positively drunk. Like, Corona and rum drunk. Now, don't think that what I did next was because I didn't love Paul; my need for male attention has nothing to do with him. I did it because I thought it would be really funny and really cool.

I cornered one of my friend Leslie's friends and convinced him to perform *Total Eclipse of the Heart* with me at karaoke night. To put it lightly, I karaoke'd the shit out of him. Embarrassed at first, we shyly swayed our hips from side to side while we sang the first verse. But by the chorus I had one leg wrapped around my new friend's waist and was mimicking a lasso motion. I think, at one point, I even dropped it like it was hot.

By the middle of the song (it is a very long song), I had noticed Laura taking pictures, which only fuelled my performance. I immediately got down on all fours and crawled towards my singing partner. Once I kitty-cat clawed my way up his chest, we both came together and pointed at the crowd while we faded out with 'Turn around ...' I collapsed in his arms as we giggled. The two of us breathlessly stumbled back to our respective friends. I turned to Laura and her boyfriend, Billy, for reassurance that what I did was cool, funny and not completely embarrassing. They swore it was epic, but I still felt a little ashamed. Not because I had danced up on another guy, but because I had just done KARAOKE. As my karaoke high wore off, I walked home, craving a figurative cigarette.

As always, the morning after shed a different light on my night of karaoke. I woke up hung-over and filled with doubt. Had I chosen the right song? Did my partner judge me? Were pictures already on Facebook? Why I couldn't just be like those amazing girls who get on stage and belt out a Zooey Deschanel song? (Oh, that's right: I can't sing, and they haven't incorporated auto-tune into karaoke microphones yet.) I swore to never have an irresponsible, one-night karaoke session again.

After vowing to swear off karaoke, I always convince myself that it would be okay if I did a group performance; it seems safe. It is not. Turns out, group karaoke is just like a public orgy.

Once, my friends and I ran to the stage after choosing *I Will Survive*. We clasped hands and fought over the microphones. Within seconds, I started focusing on one specific friend in particular (kind of hard to not play favourites in such a close and intimate setting). Thirty seconds in, we had all developed some amateur choreography; everyone was really starting to work it. The finale came from deep within our guts. We got down on our knees, raised our hands up like we were a gospel choir and belted out, 'I WILL SURVIVE, I WILL SURVIVE, I WILL SURVIVE!'

Funnily enough, the morning after that I woke up feeling just as guilty and slutty as when I was with just one singing partner. I tried to rationalise all of the girl-on-girl body rolls by thinking about the 60s and free love. I knew it was just karaoke, but there had been a lot of real emotions shared on the stage. There were obvious givers and takers, and so much eye contact and sexual tension. When I really think about it, I *had* survived. I survived a potentially risky situation: a public display of bi-curiosity by heterosexual girls.

I always have the same New Year's resolutions, one of them being that I will not partake in karaoke. The reason is simple: I feel exactly the same way after karaoke as I do after a one-night stand. You might not think that the two events are similar in the least, but when you really break it down, it's all fairly obvious. They both require confidence, aggressiveness and sexual energy; we are usually left feeling used and exposed afterwards; people talk and pictures circulate. (I cannot tell you how many times I have found a karaoke picture of myself on Facebook with an 'o-face' and a wonky eye. And I can't even play it off like I wasn't aware of the picture-taker. Not when I'm pointing directly at the camera.) No matter what, though, as you piece together the parts of your karaoke experience that you *do* remember, you will certainly have some peace and quiet to think about it. Because, just like a one-night stand, the audience does *not* call the next day.

Do:
Clean up after your Summer.

It wasn't long after my little tryst on Martha's Vineyard that I travelled back to Boston for Lisa's wedding. (Lisa is Laura's other sister.) It just so happened that I arrived on a Thursday night, which was Family Dinner Night, a ritual Laura and her friends do weekly. It was the usual: home-made pasta, pizza and eleven bottles of wine. At one point, I was using my fingers to shove prosciutto and mozzarella into my mouth, while using my toes to feed myself some vino; impressive, I know.

The next day I woke up around noon, feeling uncom-fortably full. (I'm still not sure which hangover is worse: wine or Italian food.) Regardless, I got up, cleaned the apartment and decided to go for a run. After overindulging the night before, I wanted to get outside, inhale that fresh

September air and sweat out the copious amounts of meat, cheese and alcohol that were circulating through my body.

After lapping the Boston Common and the Charles River, I was exhausted and rapidly approaching stage-three poop cramps. It was time to change direction and head back to Laura's apartment. I was exhausted and uncomfortable, but couldn't slow my pace. My quick strides were doing a decent job of muffling my farts as I ran through Faneuil Hall, one of the most populated parts of Boston. Legs aching, I clenched my butt cheeks while scampering up six flights of stairs.

Laura's house is notorious for flaky plumbing, so I went to the downstairs toilet, which was usually the most reliable. (But really, it was because it saved me from having to climb another flight of stairs and potentially crapping my pants.) I flipped the lid and noted that the water looked low, but at this point I had sweat in my eyes and was 'turtle-heading'. There was no time. Finally, I sat down, marvelled at the fact that there were no skid marks on my underwear, and dropped a solid, healthy poop. (Thanks, probiotics!) As always, I went to examine my specimen and was completely amazed by how black it was. I hoped it was just a side effect of the red wine, because that thing more closely resembled a piece of coal than human fecal matter. Feeling otherwise satisfied, I pressed on the handle to flush.

Nothing. Not even a faint whine of water trying to do its job. I looked in the tank. It was dry as the Sahara. Commence full-fledged panicking.

I instantly called Paul in Australia to explain my dilemma. (Let's be honest here, this situation merits an international call, regardless of the charges.) He told me to pour water in the bowl. So I did. No help. I ran back upstairs for a second jug, but before I had the chance to dump it in (no pun intended), he told me to check that the pipes were turned on. Once I turned the knob, my poop disappeared! Relieved, I turned the pipes back off, assuming building maintenance was fixing a leak or something. While mentally cursing them for not having the decency to leave a sign, I made sure the floor was dry and went about my day.

Around midnight, Laura sent me a text message to see what I was up to (she was already staying where the wedding was being held). I texted her the story of my plumbing issues.

With horror she texted, 'No. Oh my god, oh my god, oh my god. Noooooo.'

I replied, 'Yeah! Hahaha, don't worry. My poop went down, along with my dignity.'

She then replied, 'You are going to have to bag it.'

The horror didn't have time to set in. My phone rang; it was Laura's boyfriend, Billy.

'Summer, you are going to have to go into my closet, find the crawl space under the stairs and pick up your poo. That toilet isn't connected to anything!'

Straight face, times a thousand.

Things started to become glaringly obvious: the curious smell in the hallway I had noticed, but been too tired to investigate, the low water, the pipes. I had to take action. So I got out of bed, gathered some trash bags and cleaning wipes and searched for gloves.

No gloves. Fantastic.

While pulling out Billy's luggage and winter clothes, I thought, 'What did I do to deserve this?'

The crawl space was easy enough to find and, sure enough, my shit was there to greet me. Three little turds, all in a row. If that weren't enough, Billy had put a towel down, just in case water leaked. So I had to bag the poopy towel, along with the poopy. It took me a while to actually gather the strength to pick it up. And when I called my mom for sympathy, all I got was laughter. (Donna's toilet humour is even more on point than mine – the apple doesn't fall far from the tree.)

As I tried to gather up the stuff, I violently gagged at the less-than-inviting aroma and accidentally got a skid mark on my hand. That only intensified my disgust. Ten minutes and a hundred cleaning wipes later, I had bagged my shit and wiped the floor's ass.

I held the bag a good foot in front of me while I went down the stairs and along the street. The long walk to the garbage can on the corner was a good time for me to reflect on what had just happened. I concluded that I am still truly the grossest thing I have ever encountered. That includes dirty diapers, infections, cystic acne, Fat Bastard's poop water that Austin Powers drank and those giant cockroach piles that feed on bat poop in caves. Yup, I top 'em all. I also learned that, if the toilet water looks low, don't try to fix it. Chances are, you're not a plumber, and you will have to bag your own poop.

Oh, and the answer is yes. I did take a picture.

Do:
Say yes.

Paul decided to come for two months to wait with me while my visa was being approved[1]. Finally, 4 October was upon us and I waited in the Gainesville Regional Airport to collect Paul and fall into his arms. I tried to contain my excitement, but as soon as he was through the revolving doors I was mouth-raping him.

We spent the rest of the day cuddling, eating, snuggling, eating, laughing, lovemaking, eating and then eating more. He kept asking if we could do something super-special for dinner, but we were both so ridiculously full by 7 p.m. that we decided to call it a night. Paul was busy brushing his teeth when I called him in to my room. I was curled up in the foetal position and complaining about my stomach-ache.

'Paul, my belly hurts so badly. I think I ate way too much tempura vegetables (fffffffffahhhhhhhhtttttttt).' (In case you're wondering, that was a fart noise.) Looking as pathetic as humanly possible, I jokingly said, 'Would you marry this?'

'Why? Is this how you would want me to ask?'

'I don't know. I mean, I am just so gross.'

And then Paul walked over to his bag and got something out. He came back and got down on his knee, presented a ring and asked me to marry him. Right then and there in the waft of my fart. And yes, I said yes.

I love how Paul proposed. It was so natural and comfortable and real. I'm a farter, and could never date someone who didn't accept me for who I am. I'm also the

---

1   It was about time. If I had to Skype-seduce him one more time, I was going to kill myself. Especially after the last time. I was giving Paul a little web show when his dad walked in and saw my butt on his son's computer. Paul screamed, 'Dad just walked in!' but I was too busy shaking what Donna gave me to hear him. When I saw his father's figure approach, I did the only logical thing I could think of. I slammed my laptop shut and waited for Paul to call. Which he did. Apparently his dad said, 'That's disgusting, Paul!' He's super Christian. I'm so glad Jewish people aren't weird about sex.

grossest human being in the world, as you would probably have gathered by now.

A Donnalandish Thought on Summer and Paul:

One of the things I like most about Paul is that he can stand Summer.

Don't: Leave your used tampon where someone may find it.

It's quite embarrassing how many times some part of my tampon has been exposed. Let's just say I make Britney Spears circa 2007 look like an incredibly composed person. After a Summerlandish tampon sighting, you might actually feel more comfortable taking Tila Tequila home to meet your parents, rather than me. That little mouse tail always seems to be dangling out from my miniskirt. Or it's seen flashing from the edge of my bikini (a great look when you're shamelessly molesting the lifeguard with your intimate, predatory gaze). You might even think that I purposely put my sanitary aid on display but, unfortunately, it's just that I lack the self-awareness to appear 'put together' in public settings.

My 'exposures' are not limited to public events, however. I used to simply forget to remove my tampon before

I hopped in the shower. I ended up taking it out (so I could wash my female parts without it soaking up all of the soap) and tossing the cottontail in the soap dish. Of course, I would always make a mental note to throw it away. But, seven times out of ten, my mom or brother would come barging into my room a few minutes later. They'd interrupt my ritual of peeling all the skin off my feet and scream, 'SUMMER, WHAT THE FUCK!? YOUR BLOODY TAMPON IS STAINING THE SHOWER WALL!' Then they'd usually proceed to gag and walk away. Filled with shame, I always got up immediately to remove it. To be fair, it wasn't like I'd meant to leave it in the shower! Cut me some slack, family. (And really, Donna, it's technically your own blood … if you think about it.)

Having your brother find your tampon is one level of embarrassment. And, of course, it is also mildly awkward and horrible when your boyfriend finds it in an unflushed toilet. But the ultimate humiliation is when your friend's dad happens upon your used Tampax.

This occurred when I went over to Megan's house to play in her pool. I was in the eighth grade and had only gotten my period about six months earlier, so I was really into it. Not willing to accept that my cycle had ended for the month, I continued to wear a 'just in case' tampon. The precaution resulted in that horrible cramping feeling you get when you have a dry tampon in a dry vagina. (If you're a male, you'll just have to trust me.)

So, in between cannon balls and swan dives, I pulled my tampon out (not bloody) and put it on the side of the pool. Once again, I made a mental note to throw it away when we were done swimming. (I was not yet aware of the fact that I have absolutely no short-term memory.) We finished playing Marco Polo, and I went home.

Around the time I was finishing dinner, Megan's dog was sniffing her way around the pool. Sophie, the little Shih tzu, picked up that regular-absorption tampon and trotted over to Megan's dad. Roger was minding his own business, reading on their porch, when the pup carefully gifted her findings onto his lap. Being a good dog, Sophie proceeded to request a treat for her good deed. In utter shock, disgust and amazement, Megan's dad immediately called his wife to 'deal with the situation'. It was eventually discovered that I had been the culprit. (Megan obviously dobbed me in with a 'Summer did it!' response.) Afterwards, I was not able to look Roger in the eyes for a week. (Which is DECADES in kid years.)

After Paul and I got engaged we had an extremely intoxicated night out of town and decided to go home (to our friend's house) so we could make sweet, passionate love. It's funny; you can always manage to feel sexy after drinking your body weight in champagne, even when you are haemorrhaging from your vagina. I ended up ripping my tampon out and throwing it into the darkness of the guest bedroom. The next morning, I woke up with a deathly hangover and a panic attack; our flight was taking off in just two hours. After throwing our stuff into suitcases, we ran out the door. The plane ended up being delayed, which resulted in Paul and me eating overpriced sandwiches at the airport, where we waited for seven hours. Our friend had been calling to check up on our flight status, which was fine and somewhat thoughtful; then the phone rang because of something else. She had found my used tampon on her white carpet and screamed, 'ARE YOU KIDDING ME? IT WAS STILL WARM WHEN I PICKED IT UP!' Once again, I felt awkward and horrible. (Although I think the 'still warm' detail had been exaggerated. I mean, come on, it had been *hours*.)

It would be some saving grace to say that these events only transpired in the privacy of other people's homes. But I once removed a tampon while shuffling through the crowds at the University of Florida's Swamp Stadium. The lines for the bathroom were ginormous, and I had experienced the initial gush of the Tampax dam breaking. I removed the tampon, tucked it into the outer pocket of my bag and quickly plugged up Old Faithful with a new one. Roughly thirty minutes later, Paul and I were bored with football and ventured to the bars to meet up with our friends. As soon as we arrived, Hillary noticed a suspicious stain on the outside of my purse. Yes, the blood was leaking through. I freaked out (it was a brand-new Longchamp bag) and grabbed the tampon. Hillary and I made eye contact and then simultaneously looked at my clinched fist, then back at each other. In pure panic mode, I hurled my tampon behind the cigarette machine, doused my hand in vodka and begged her not to commit me to a mental institution.

Looking back on all of this, I feel like I owe a few people some apologies. It seems like my family, close friends, and the city of Gainesville have suffered the most. I am sorry, Donna. I am sorry, Brett. I am sorry, Megan and Roger. I am sorry, Hillary and Paul. And I am very sorry, bar (which shall not be named but will figure it out when they move their cigarette machine). I wish I could say that the story ends here, and that I figured out how to use tampons in a discreet manner. But that would be a lie. There is one final transgression to mention.

Fast-forward to that December when I finally got my visa and Paul and I moved to Wollongong and got an apartment. Six months later it was moving day yet again. (Paul's main goal at the time was to get a job as a fitter in a coal mine and, since he had no experience, we'd have to move all the way to Mudgee for him to get a job and pay his dues.)

Of course, I was too busy to help move. (I had to get my hair coloured, since I can't pull off the Carrie Bradshaw regrowth look. If I try, it ends up looking like I'm from a trailer park and should be wearing a Mickey Mouse or Tweety Bird shirt.) In my absence, Paul, his dad and his friends decided to move the furniture first.

As you might expect, they dumped all of the stuff from our dressers into the middle of the floor. When I walked in I greeted the boys, as well as my purple vibrator (aka the Rabbit), which was lying on the floor. Nostrils flared, I quickly put it in my purse and bitched out Paul. Next, I stormed back into our room, looked at the remaining pile of crap and started packing. I noticed a piece of wood on the floor and flashed back to when I knocked my laptop off our dresser and broke the handle off one of the drawers. (Hope his dad hadn't noticed it, as he had built the dresser with his own hands.)

As the junk pile got smaller, I looked at the wood again and thought, 'No, that looks more like a stick from outside.' But I ignored it and continued working. Twenty minutes later, all that was left on the floor was garbage. I picked up the stick, and quickly recoiled as I realised that it was a petrified used tampon. Even the string was stiff and dried out. Not only had Paul's friends and family seen my massive purple vibrating bunny penis, they had also seen my dried bloody tampon. I told Paul and my friend, Molly, who was also over, and they admitted that neither of them had known what it was. So I was saved from embarrassment … this time.

I thought about including photographic evidence (yes, I took a picture) but I figured I should spare you. It's bad enough that I have countless people to apologise to for various tampon exposures; I don't feel like adding everyone who reads this book to that list, too.

Don't:
Poop
where you
shouldn't.

While I did scar Paul with my period blood and near-lethal farts, he scarred me with ... well, let's just start at the beginning. It was a hot and humid October afternoon in Gainesville. Paul decided to challenge the impressively ferocious weather. He boldly decided to go for a run to the University of Florida's stadium (aka the Swamp). The plan was for a two-mile run followed by a 45-minute workout, and a return run home. I declined when he enthusiastically asked me to join. Being all too familiar with the suffocating heat of Florida, I opted for an indoor, air-conditioned gym class with Hillary instead.

About an hour later, I came home to find Paul, showered and doing laundry. He grabbed both of my hands and sat me down.

'Something happened.'

I rapidly entered panic mode. We were in Australian visa waiting mode, so I asked if he had received a call about it. Paul responded, 'No, no, nothing like that.'

And so, deflated, I listened to his tale. For full effect, I'll let Paul tell it:

I was running to the stadium and everything was going fine. I felt really strong. Around University Avenue I started getting some unnatural gurgles in my stomach and instinctively knew that I needed to find a bathroom in the worst way possible. I looked at the shops and bars, but thought I probably had to buy something to use their facilities. I had no cash on me and didn't really feel like screaming at a cashier that I was about to have explosive diarrhoea. I knew that I would not make it across the street without an anal explosion happening. So I decided to go behind a dumpster that was (thank God) surrounded by a fence. As students rode their Vespas and fixed-speed road bikes by me, I ripped the most massive fart in the world. A force of wind broke through my shorts as I exhaled with relief. I was confident that I could make it the next thirty metres to the stadium to use the bathroom. Twenty-eight metres later, the pain started again. I was only seconds away from being inside the stadium when my stomach screamed at me, 'ggggggggggrrrrrrrrrb-blllllllllllameeeeeeeechaaaaaaaaaaaaaaaaaaabooooooop'.

I ducked into an alcove that was home to the janitor's closet, went in the corner and pulled my pants down. Before I could even squat, a grapefruit-sized ball of sloppy poop shot out of my arse and spray-painted the wall. Not a single drip hit the ground. I removed my undies, wiped my bum the best I could and left them under my wall art. I was so exhausted and in shock from the war my arse just had with the wall that I slowly walked into the Swamp and cleaned myself up in the bathroom.

Funny how you cannot really get the poop smell off without a good shower! After my millionth paper towel, I tucked my tail between my legs and walked home. Because of the heat, my legs and faeces were creating the perfect environment for chafing. I had a mixture of blood, sweat and poop wrestling between my thighs. Not to mention, a soiled pair of board shorts.

Paul finished his story and held my gaze while he desperately searched my face for a response. As I stood with my arms akimbo and my mouth agape, I looked into Paul's eyes and knew that there was really only one thing to say: 'Can we go see it???'

We applied some cream to his poop-rashed thighs, got in the car and drove to the stadium. After parking around back, I was so excited that I was skipping. As we drew closer to the historical man-mark, we froze in our tracks. SOMEONE WAS TAKING A PHOTO OF IT. Paul stopped dead, grabbed my hand and slowly guided me away. 'We have to go, we have to go' he hissed. In fear of getting caught and being charged with vandalism with bodily excrement, we switched our direction and sprinted for the car. Although we were laughing all the way, I was devastated that I didn't get a picture. I could have made millions with it at the next year's Art Basel in Miami.

So, please, consider this an open letter to that man who was aiming a camera at Paul's 'art'. Dear Mr Poop Photographer, if you still have the picture of the wall poop, please email it to hello@summerlandish.com. I will be forever grateful. And I have no doubt that our kids will thank you too.

LESSONS LEARNT WHEN YOU LIVE HAPPILY EVER AFTER

After six months of living in my hometown, during which I experienced a raging case of shingles, ate approximately fifty-three sushi rolls and made countless visits to the gym with Hillary, the Australian government finally granted me a visa to live in Australia with my one true love.

Do:
Move to a
new country.

I did my best to fit all of my belongings into four suitcases, but was fighting a mental battle as to whether to bring all of my American Girl dolls and their trunks, wardrobes and books, or just my Beanie Baby collection. After Paul convinced me over the phone (he was already back in Australia) that we could ship them when we have kids, I used my body weight to close my overstuffed bags and zipped them shut.

Donna and Emily, who had been visiting, took me to the airport. Even though I was ready to start my life with Paul Down Under, I couldn't help but put on a Sea World–worthy show of waterworks for my mom. I was moving far away and we'd have to pay international call rates to communicate, not to mention we'd be on completely opposite schedules. So I cried and got an extra-long mom hug from Donna.

Saying goodbye to Emily, on the other hand, was easier. Not that I love her any less, but because I knew that she'd come visit all the time; she loves Australia. And me. Plus, she was flying back to Boston, so we had some extra gate time. After we waved goodbye to Donna, we hit up Starbucks for some iced soy chai lattes and went into a Hudson News. I checked out the bestsellers section right away.

As Emily browsed the business book section and picked up *The New Rules of Marketing and PR* by David Meerman Scott, I stared at an array of Emily Giffin novels and thought, 'I want nothing more than to have my book sold in an airport.' A few months earlier, Emily had built my blog, www.summerlandish.com, and I had been posting stories. But the more I wrote, the more I wanted to write a book. As I stood there, gazing at the number-one spot, I set a goal: Write a book that is worthy of being sold in an airport. And that is possibly in the number-one spot. And has a really cool cover. And has awesome reviews on the back.

Since Emily and I love vision boards and goals, I immediately wrote my new goal in my notebook and made a note to add a photo of Hudson News to my vision board when I got to Australia.

Before we knew it, it was time for me to go. I hugged the crap out of Emily and was off to LAX. I left LAX on 23 December, but arrived in Sydney on 25 December; the 24th was taken from me. I mean, I guess I experienced a couple of hours of it, but not enough to feel like I got my daily intake of that day, per se. I couldn't complain too hard, though; at least it wasn't my birthday or anything. And I was about to see Paul!

Customs seemed to take extra-long, as did my wait at baggage claim. Finally, my fourth bag rolled around and I loaded up my cart. I hastily pushed my way through all of the other arriving passengers and went to find Paul. I scanned the crowds in Sydney's international terminal: couples kissing, families hugging and backpackers staring at maps, but no Paul. Just as I went to find a payphone, I noticed a man dressed as Santa holding a rose. I was surprised that the airport had hired a Santa for Christmas; airports are not really known for embracing festive occasions. I silently prayed that he wouldn't come over – I was exhausted, and not in the Christmas spirit. I kept trying to avoid eye contact, but Santa just kept getting closer and closer. And this was a poor man's Santa, if you asked me. He was pretty skinny and wearing flip-flops. Wait a minute. He was PAUL.

Of all the ways I had imagined our reunion, I did *not once* picture him dressed as the one and only Santa Claus. I couldn't help but jump into his arms, red suit or not, and plant a huge kiss right on his mouth, unbrushed teeth and all. He spun me around (just like in the movies) and then we pushed my luggage to the car.

We moved in with his mom until we both got jobs. Paul was searching for a machinist/fitter job in a coalmine, and I was looking for something in the marketing field. After a week, we felt a little discouraged so I suggested that we write down our goals for that year. (I'm all about manifesting my own destiny.)

GOALS (in no particular order):

Get jobs
Get an apartment
Get iPhones
Get cars
Save $35,000

Rather quickly, things fell into place. I got a job working as the marketing manager for a cosmetics company, and Paul started contracting for the steelworks. We bought a $300 car[1]. Next, we got an apartment a block from the beach. Paul spent his days off swimming and periodically getting stung by bluebottle jellyfish. I stuck to dry land and joined a group-fitness group called Savvy. I also started making some really awesome friends. (Turns out there are a tonne of Americans living in Australia. I don't know why, but I thought I was the only one and that I was really special. But nope; there was already a club. Oh well, at least I'm a part of it now.)

Even though we had cars, jobs, an apartment and iPhones, Paul wasn't doing what he really wanted. And we definitely weren't going to be able to save $35,000 with him working as a contract employee. So he started to look outside of Wollongong for a job. By April, he had an offer. Only

---

1   Nope, I'm not missing a zero. My car was $300, and she was amazing. I called her Operation Desert Storm because she was gold with a tan interior, and could and would take me anywhere I needed to go.

problem: it was four and a half hours away in a little town known as Mudgee.

Don't:
Lose an eye.

Sometimes you have to do things that you really don't want to do. For my brother, it was eating meat at our grandmother's dinner table once a year, even though he was a vegetarian. ('Was' being the key word. At age fifteen he tasted a Slim Jim and became a carnivore once again. Damn processed meat sticks.) For me, it was moving for Paul's job. Mudgee was to add two more to its population of 12,000, all so Paul could be a fitter in a coalmine. While driving to our new life, Paul went over all of the exciting things we would be doing. He explained that I would need a fascinator for the horseraces, a swimsuit for water skiing and (oh, by the way) sunglasses, because the magpies were really aggressive in spring. *Say what???*

After clarifying that a magpie was a bird, and not a delicious Australian dessert, Paul explained, 'Yeah, you have to be careful when you're walking because the magpies are really territorial and sometimes swoop down at you this time of year. On average, two people lose their eye every season, from magpies.'

That was definitely an interesting statistic, but I didn't get further into it. I was too preoccupied, fantasising about the ostentatious fascinators I would be wearing. It was just so Kate Middleton! I immediately made Paul detour so I could go and find a headpiece. There were so many elements to consider: colour scheme, feathers, jewels, fastenings, etc. The one I ended up getting was a light-pink feather piece with pearl detailing. It was very 20s flapper girl! I LOVED it.

We finally arrived and I discovered that Mudgee is actually a very cute town. It's nestled in the hills; kangaroos rest in the paddocks that surround the city limits, and Church Street is bustling with country folk. Did I mention the multitude of wineries around? It would be the perfect place to write my memoir, with a glass of red in one hand and a cute marsupial at my feet. After unpacking my stuff into the tiniest room of all time (it was so small that I felt like a hoarder; I kept telling myself that rich people are probably hoarders too, but they just don't realise it because they have so much space) I decided to go for a walk into town. I couldn't help but feel like Julia Roberts in *Steel Magnolias*. I imagined going to the beauty parlour and gossiping with Dolly Parton about the new mayor's son. It was turning out that, despite my apprehensions, life in the Australian countryside would be so picturesque. I do declare!

Walking through the park and listening to Matchbox 20 on my iPod (not guilty), I heard a strange noise. A noise that was not to be mistaken for the backup singers on the song '3 AM'. No, this wasn't a human's voice. This was cawing. Evil cawing.

I looked to my right and noticed two magpies closing in on me. I quickly picked up my pace. 'Don't lose an eye,' I told myself. Cornered, frightened and alone, I felt something slam into my head. It was a lot like the time my brother threw his Puma sneaker at me. But I knew that was no Puma. That was a magpie! I was being attacked! With a quick check to make sure I still had my eyeballs, I glued my hands to my sunglasses. I even curled my fingers in around the frames, in fear of losing a phalanx. Who knew what those little black-and-white pests were capable of?

Panicking, I tried to remember everything Paul had told me in the car. I think he said not to look up, because that was when the magpie could get my eye. So, naturally, I started running to the nearest street with my hands over my face. How I did not fall, I have no idea. With my back-pack on, I must have looked like a high-school freshman who was late for class; all I needed was a school map to complete the look of the biggest dork in the world.

I was engulfed by an all-consuming fear for the next three blocks. Everywhere I looked, a magpie was waiting to attack. Even as I got to town, those little fuckers were casing the streets for my whereabouts. Were they working together against me? I kept thinking that Alfred Hitchcock had probably had a run-in with a magpie. Every now and then, I checked the back of my head for dangling pieces of brain.

Luckily, I escaped with only two minor gashes and a dab of blood. (If anyone asks, it was a lot of blood.) I ended up finding a refuge in the form of a coffee shop. Breathless and high on adrenaline, I took a seat next to a young boy and his mother. Without missing a beat, I explained (in detail) everything that had just happened to me. (I don't remember if they even asked, but this magpie attack was a perfect opportunity to get to know some people.) They told me to wear a hat with googly eyes on the top of it. Apparently, if you constantly look up at magpies, they will not attack.

I knew that deciding to move to Australia meant that I had chosen a country with some of the most deadly creatures on the planet. I have to constantly check my shoes for funnel-web spiders and dodge tall grass due to fear of brown snakes. When swimming in the ocean, I always wear a wetsuit just in case a jellyfish the size of my fingernail decides to try to kill me. And I am very aware of the treacherous crocodiles, dingoes and drunken Australian men lurking up north. I had come to terms with all of this. But I was *not* ready for the whole magpie thing.

I cried to Paul that I needed to move home and that I hated it in Mudgee. He told me that I had to stick it out for at least a year, at least until he could get enough experience in a mine to move back to Wollongong or Sydney.

If living in Mudgee meant living with Paul, I'd take one for the team. Even if it meant trading in my fascinator for a protective helmet with googly eyes.

Do:
Get a new
best friend.

I had been in Mudgee about a month when I escaped to Sydney for a little weekend getaway. I went to visit my friends Vickers and Josh to get some much-needed polluted air. It's not that I don't love the country; it's just that I love public transportation. I also love brownstone apartments, city parks and free wi-fi.

When I came home on the Sunday, I was invigorated, inspired and ready to write my book and cuddle up to Paul. We got in the car and headed to Woolworths to restock the fridge. Paul and I happened to be walking through the pet aisle of the grocery store. At that moment, I decided to share my feelings about getting a canine. 'You know what? I don't want a dog. I love that we can run away every weekend and don't have to worry about a dog depending on us for food and shelter.' As Paul was agreeing, my new friend Erin called and asked me to coffee. Feeling especially free, I abandoned Paul at the store to go meet up with her.

When I walked into the cafe, she looked up and said, 'I have a surprise for you ...' I was secretly hoping that she was going to tell me she was pregnant. Nope, not pregnant. But she did have something to show me in a laundry basket under the table. When I peered inside and pulled back a little fleece blanket, I saw the CUTEST little puppy I had ever seen. Apparently her golden retriever had knocked up a kelpie from her husband's family's farm. The pup's mother had unexpectedly died. So tragic. She went on to explain that the farmhands were just going to 'knock him over the head with a shovel'. So, you see, I HAD TO TAKE THE LITTLE GUY.

I admit it. I am not a 'dog person'. Believe me, I've tried. I grew up with two pups and once even bought a $700 chihuahua with Donna's credit card.

I was in high school and on the hunt for a canine companion. When I was at the counter paying for him, I briefly considered consulting Donna about it. After all, this was a rather serious purchase. But then the pet store clerk said, 'It's easier to ask for forgiveness than permission.' What a salesman! With that, I was convinced that it was totally the best decision ever, and I became a new mommy. It didn't even take two hours for Donna and me to return the puppy. I freaked out, cried, apologised for not asking permission and told her I wasn't responsible enough to take care of it, all topped off with a 'please take it back'.

It was a turning point in my life. It became clear to me that I was way too immature and selfish to own a dog ... or goldfish, turtle, bird, horse or any living creature, for that matter. (Unfortunately, it wasn't until much later in life that I learned I was also way too immature and selfish to even own a credit card.) I don't know why I impulsively decided to buy a chihuahua that day. I don't even think they're cute. I guess it was a combination of *The Simple Life* being really popular at the time and the fact that reality television was a heavy influence in my life. Plus, whenever Donna or I say, 'I'm just going to look,' we always end up leaving with a new car, animal and/or timeshare. (Lesson learned: when it comes to timeshares, just take the free cruise and get out.)

About eight years prior to the four-hour chihuahua incident, the Land family impulsively rescued two dogs. We named them Calvin and Tess. Brett and I swore we would walk and feed them every day. Well, that lasted for *one* day. After that, Donna went through the same rite of passage that every mother goes through when they get their child a pet: she became the sole caretaker, for the next twelve years.

I can see how this was stressful for her. Calvin and Tess barked constantly, and they shed on everything. Since Cesar Millan wasn't on the scene yet, and there was no such thing as an online forum, my mom didn't know how to deal with the incessant barking that was about to get us kicked out of the neighbourhood. Citronella collars didn't work because Calvin and Tess actually liked getting shot in the face with orange-flavoured spray. So Donna turned to shock collars, but the dogs figured out how to bark in a sequence that threw off the sensor. (My brother and his friends did not figure it out; they got shocked every time they put them on.)

After countless attempts to make our dogs shut the hell up, Donna finally broke down and did the only thing she could think of: she had their vocal cords removed. (Can you say 'dog Nazi'?) You should have heard their muted barking efforts. It sounded like an old man with emphysema trying to get your attention, which made them seem endearing and wise, in a way.

Now, I don't want you to think that Calvin and Tess weren't loved. They were. Donna showered them with hugs and doggy biscuits. Brett would dye Calvin's fur green so that he was always the coolest dog on the block. And I always let them eat my scrunchies, socks and underwear. So you see, the pooches actually lived long and happy doggy lives. Eventually, they died of old age and were buried in Donna's yard.

Having those dogs helped me realise that I don't really like having dogs. They mostly made me feel guilty every time I stopped petting them or didn't take them for a walk. I also don't usually like other people's dogs because they just take the attention away from me. And, after nearly being mauled by a German shepherd as a child, I sure as hell don't like that breed, especially. (Bringing the tally of things I am deathly afraid of to three: roaches, whipper snippers and German shepherds.)

Yup, my getting a dog was just about as unplanned as a teenage pregnancy. But my maternal instincts must have been on steroids, because as soon as I held my little bundle of joy, all of my regrets and apprehensions faded away. My newly orphaned puppy was twelve days old, couldn't walk and hadn't even opened his eyes yet. We named him Cooper. I hurried home and put him on my bare belly so that we could have skin-to-skin contact; he needed to learn my scent as soon as possible. I found myself sleep-deprived from feeding him at two-hour intervals and leaning over my bed to peer into his laundry basket. It seemed like I could watch his little tummy move up and down for hours on end.

One morning, around 5 a.m., I woke up with the maternal instinct that Cooper wasn't in his basket. Carefully, I crept towards the light switch and flicked it on. Sure enough, the basket was empty. I began checking under the bed and behind the nightstand. Nothing. Panic was creeping in when I finally spotted his little tail. He had buried himself inside one of my ugg boots. It was the most adorable thing I had ever seen. I ended up giving him the boot later that day. Of course, it didn't occur to me that he would actually wedge himself down into the toe. When that happened, I had to bust out my scissors and destroy the thing just to get him out. Regardless, I'd let him eat my Chanel handbag if he wanted (well, if I had one).

As the weeks flew by, Cooper went from nursing one bottle to chugging down more bottles than a frat dog. He loved long walks on the beach and was becoming quite the retriever. I decked him out in the cutest dog collars and did daily affirmations with him. I would look him straight in the eye and say, 'You are loved, you are amazing and you can be anything you want to be when you grow up.'

I happily spent every waking moment with Cooper, even trading in bar time for barking time. One night, I had some friends over for dinner. Erin brought up that spitting in your dog's mouth would make them loyal to you forever. I immediately called Cooper over and spat in his mouth. Not a loogie or anything, but enough that he had to swallow it. When I looked up, there were six people staring at me. Including Paul. I suddenly felt super-weird about it, like I had just done something wrong. But can you really blame me for wanting to do everything in my power to make Cooper feel like he is a part of me?

Paul did. He blamed me, good. He thought it was trashy.

Whatever, clearly I loved Cooper more than he did. After all, I was the one who filled out the dog papers and named him Cooper Land at his first vet appointment. Of course, Paul was horrified that I used my maiden name.

It's not that I didn't want him to get any credit for our puppy-child, but what kind of name is Cooper Jongsma? I flipped out when I found out that Paul had gone to the vet and changed Cooper's name to just that and said that it had to at least be Cooper Land-Jongsma. We argued for a solid ten minutes until Paul finally admitted that he was just joking: he hadn't actually changed Cooper's name. It's a good thing, too. He had no right to make that change. I mean, he hadn't even spat in Cooper's mouth.

Owning a dog with someone is challenging. But it's the perfect way to see what kind of parent someone is going to be. Obviously, I'm going to probably eat my baby's placenta and harvest its stem cells. Paul, on the other hand, has really surprised me. He willingly pays $60 a week for Cooper to go to Doggersize. This gives me hope for my whole private-school argument for our future kids.

Don't:
Try this
at home.

What with mothering Cooper, I was a busy lady – and as a result, I started neglecting my personal grooming a bit. Since Australia has opposite seasons, I spent the Christmas and Jewish holidays lying out by the pool. One day I looked down and saw that my bikini line was completely out of control and emotionally scarring little children. I decided I needed to take action IMMEDIATELY. I stopped by a Big W on my way home and picked up some wax strips.

Now, I probably should have known better. Megan once sealed her butt cheeks together with wax when she was trying to do a little at-home hair removal. We ended up having to use canola oil to get them apart. That would have been fine, except her dad came looking for the canola a few days later and was a bit disturbed when we told him it was in her bathroom ... covered in waxing strips and pubes. Next, my mom called me in a tizzy because she had glued her vagina lips together with wax. After avoiding losing a lip and getting them apart, I swore up and down that I would NEVER try to wax at home.

But this was an emergency! The moment I arrived home and got started, I called Mama Donna and told her that I was waxing my bikini line as we spoke. Well, I was halfway there. I had the strip on, but couldn't work up the nerve to pull it off. Trying to stay positive, I figured that the amount I was sweating would help remove it easily. Unfortunately, I just couldn't work up any courage to finish my task. Donna was cheering me on, but I ended up calling for Paul to come and help me get it off. (I was sitting in the living room, of course.) He came in and held me down while I burst into tears. My mom was howling with laughter as Paul told me not to be such a baby and ripped the wax strip, along with all of the blood vessels, off my delicate inner-thigh area.

Trying to nurse my injury was particularly horrible because Christmas 2011 in Australia was a hot one. Not that the entire season was particularly sweltering, but Christmas Day was a joke. I went to bed in the nude and rapidly became dehydrated from sweating so much. Paul switched the extremely old ceiling fan to high, which, in turn, added a nice clicking/whomping soundtrack to our sleep session. I was too hot to care that the fan looked like it could, at any point, lose its grip on the ceiling and come down on us. Paul and I surprisingly managed to fall asleep (more or less pass out, from lack of fluids) for about two hours before waking up to complain about the fucking fan being so fucking loud. (I'm cranky when I don't get sleep.) Paul turned it off, but there was still a noise that was so irritating that I had to say something.

'Paul! Stop rattling your foot.'

'I thought that was you …'

SILENCE.

The sobering reality set in that neither of us was making the sound of something crawling over the abundance of crap on our bedroom floor. We started to panic. Who was the third party? I quietly told Paul to turn the light on. Paul quietly told me that he would have to fix the light bulb. As he fumbled with the 60s lampshade and screwed in the new bulb, it began to flicker. Then we heard a dark, evil scratching noise. We looked at each other and said, in unison, 'It's a mouse!'

I was thrilled because I love rodents. (I once had a pet rat named Lucy. Sadly, after spending $600 in veterinary fees to fix her teeth, Donna had to have her put her down.) Paul, on the other hand, was less than thrilled. He knew how difficult it would be to capture and/or kill this varmint. Finally, the light flickered on completely and illuminated our bedroom.

It was not a mouse. It was my absolute biggest fear: a cockroach, aka Lucifer, the Demon Roach of 2011.

We watched as Lucifer tried (and failed) to crawl up our wall. He was so big that his substantial weight kept pulling him back down to our mortal world. When he noticed Paul coming to smash him (with MY phone) he stood up on his hind legs and emitted what can only be described as a purely evil sound. I burst into tears as Paul summoned his inner 'old priest and young priest' to fight this devilish insect. I couldn't help but think about the fact that I had just recently hung my leg off the bed because I was so hot. What if Lucifer had crawled over my foot?! Amputation would've been the only option.

Finally, Paul slammed my iPhone down on the beast. Instead of thanking my hero and rejoicing, I started freaking out because he'd used my iPhone. I mean, I'd only had my iPhone on my vision board one year prior!

With Lucifer banished to the Porcelain Hell down the hall, Paul and I began to recap every horrific moment of what we had just experienced. I probably sound crazy, I know. But the good news is that I get to blame Donna for all of this. She *also* has a completely irrational fear of cockroaches. Therefore, obviously, she raised me to be the same way. It probably wasn't intentional, but I grew up mimicking her shrill scream and tippy-toe dance whenever one of the little fuckers would scurry through the kitchen. To her credit, she has been trying her hardest to overcome the debilitating phobia. She started touching images of roaches and has even kissed a picture of one of them, on a Raid can, in Wal-Mart. (Don't tell, but I check peopleofwalmart.com for pictures of Donna every day.)

For my mom, though, the fear extends to other crawlers, such as spiders. Not me. I could make out with a tarantula and enjoy it. But I remember Donna was even afraid to make play-spiders out of egg cartons and pipe cleaners as a preschool teacher. Crazy, right? So I guess I should be somewhat happy that my fear is 100 per cent monogamous to cockroaches. I think it's their speed that's intimidating. That and their outfits (the wings, legs and feelers) are just so dominatrix. Maybe if they just slowed down a bit and got cute puffer jackets, I could make peace.

Until then, I am just not interested in a friendship. I feel like people are always buzzing in my ear about my need to get over my fear of roaches. I say screw that. They are evil and need to stay out of my house. I mean, I wouldn't ask the students at Hogwarts to get over their fear of He-Who-Must-Not-Be-Named. To be honest, I think the real issue here is people who *don't* fear roaches. How can they trust one of the only things that would supposedly survive a nuclear apocalypse? Don't they get it? THERE IS NO WAY TO PERMANENTLY ELIMINATE THEM! None.

LESSONS LEARNT
WHEN YOU REFLECT

After being in Australia for a year, I decided to do an audit of my life. I was in love, had recently purchased a house and had a dog. But I was still feeling unsatisfied. What was I missing? A career? Well, yes, but I was working on that part. Was I drinking too much? (Possibly, because I was in outback Australia and that was basically the only hobby available.)

Don't:
Drink
(caffeine)
and drive.

One day, I stumbled upon my old Emerson folders. I looked through my past homework assignments and got the idea that maybe I needed to do a SWOT analysis on myself. It was quite revealing.

STRENGTHS	WEAKNESSES
- Motivated	- Impatient
- Hard-working	- Ill-tempered
- Kind	- Selfish
- Super-flexible	- Not physically strong
- Multiple party tricks	- Nail biter
- Well-travelled	- Rarely brushes hair
- List writer	- Farts in front of boys
- Knows most movie quotes	- Hides boogers in armpit
- Tech savvy	- Horrible with cell phones (break/ loss)
- Educated	- Scared of roaches, German shepherds and whipper snippers
- Not afraid of rodents or spiders	
OPPORTUNITIES	THREATS
- Writing	- Caffeine
- Family	- Drugs
- Travel	- Anxiety
- Love	- Untreated OCD and/or ADHD
- Laughter	- Poor money management
- Personal trainer	- Love of A&E reality television
- Dance instructor	- Homesickness
- Actor	- Food poisoning (never fully cooks chicken)
- Mother	

Let's look further into my top three threats, shall we?

Seeing as I am from the South, you would think that I could suck down sweet tea while simultaneously dazzling the world of debutantes with my composure and grace. Unfortunately, if I even look at a piece of chocolate or a can of Coke, or touch a coffee bean, the caffeine instantly implants itself into the base of my spine. It spreads through my body like bad ideas through the cast of *Teen Mom*. Then I magically transform into the girl at the Junior

League[1] luncheon, sucking on her strand of pearls in the corner of the room and rocking back and forth while talking to herself.

I first noticed my caffeine intolerance right before college. Never a coffee or soft-drink fan, I didn't have any known substance abuse issues yet. But on a road trip from California to Florida with Sarah, we made the epic decision to drive straight through. With no exposure to hard drugs, we opted to try Red Bull to make this 4800-kilometre trek in one go. It was about halfway through New Mexico when we looked at each other and realised that we were both wearing a poncho-sombrero combination and had been listening to Johnny Cash (on a cassette tape) for the past two hours. To top it off, there was a pile of crunched-up jumbo Red Bull cans at our feet. I started to feel really dizzy and had to pull over. I yelled at Sarah to take my sombrero off – it felt like I had eagle talons digging into my skull – but she said I already had it in my lap. After forcing down some water and eating a bag of Munchies Snack Mix, I pulled myself together and got back onto the I-10.

Since it's an approximate seventeen-hour journey across Texas, and since we hadn't learned anything from the previous few hours, we decided to load up on some more Red Bull. Texas is awesome because the speed limit is 80 miles per hour, and there is honestly nobody else on the road. The landscape reminded me of the wallpaper borders you see in American doctors' offices. They repeat every two feet: land, rock, truck stop, land, rock, truck stop. Yet my wallpaper scenery was abruptly interrupted when we

---

[1] The Junior League is 'an organisation of women committed to providing voluntarism, developing the potential of women and improving communities through the effective action and leadership of trained volunteers. Its purpose is exclusively educational and charitable.' But really it's about who has the cutest lap-dog or pastel headband and seeing who's the most ladylike.

drove by the shell of a minivan that was engulfed in flames. With nobody around, and having no clue how to extinguish a fire of that size, we kept driving. I checked my rear-view mirror to take another look at the burning van. That's when I saw a twister and completely lost it. Enter full-on Red Bull paranoia panic mode. We figured we should call the police to see if there were any tornado warnings. (Never mind the burning car.) If this was really happening, we were going to need a belt, a water pipe and Bill Paxton, stat!

After getting off the phone with the police, I realised that I probably sounded like an Arizona teenager going through an I'm-really-angry-at-my-parents-and-the-world-so-I-am-going-to-do-meth phase. There were absolutely no tornado warnings. I had probably just seen a cloud. In other words, I was out of my damn mind. Had we even seen a burning car? Or were they just caffeine-fuelled hallucinations?

I told Sarah we needed to sleep, so we stopped at a Days Inn and promptly fell into mild comas. After what we now refer to as The Red Bull Blackout of 2005, we got back on the road to finish our journey home. I threw up once on the I-75, but, other than that, we more or less got there alive.

I stayed away from Red Bull for a while. But once I got to college, I relied on it for those long library sessions and 10 a.m. 'early start' classes. (I'm not even going to fully delve into detail about what happened when I mixed Red Bull with Adderall. Short version: immediate diarrhoea; me transcribing a five-pound astronomy textbook, word-for-word, into a notebook; cleaning my entire apartment with a bottle of bleach; and rearranging the clothes in my closet in rainbow order.)

Anyway, like most girls who identify with a good Rob Reiner film, I, of course, had a 'Harry' in my life during college. We met while car-pooling to NYC together and, at the time, we did not get along at all. But one day he and I had a meaningful conversation via gchat and became friends. I'd fake orgasms in restaurants and he'd give me backhanded compliments. We took trips to museums together to talk about art. Things got to the point where 'Harry' and I would have platonic sleepovers after staying up so late to discuss the meaning of life.

Of course, this is *my* version of the story. *His* version is a little bit different. It would go something like this: I led him on for months and jerked him around by sporadically getting back together with my ex-boyfriend. Every platonic sleepover was just me being a massive tease and driving him insane. Over time, we tried to be intimate twice. The first time he couldn't get it up. The second time I called him by my ex's name. The end.

Our relationship ended dramatically when he got a girlfriend. And suddenly, I was desperately in love with my 'Harry' (aka Marc Finn). I morphed all of our non-sexual, mundane memories into a beautiful love story that Rob Reiner would direct one day. It was during a Red Bull + 5-Hour Energy 'study session' that I poured my heart and soul out to him in an email. With a glistening tear in my eye, I proofread all 1347 words that detailed every single reason why we should be together. I confessed how I loved him, even though I called him by the wrong name and was afraid of his uncircumcised penis. Once satisfied, I typed in his email address (it was even more of a sign that we were meant to be together, since I knew it by heart) and pressed send.

No response … from *him*. I did, however, get a nice reply from one of his professors who shared his first initial and last name. She, of course, did not share my feelings of love but politely pointed out that I had the wrong email address. HOW COULD I HAVE POSSIBLY TYPED THE WRONG EMAIL ADDRESS? Turned out, I had missed a 'j'. This was probably the only time in my life where my caffeine intolerance actually saved me. By the time I got the response from the nice professor, my caffeine high had worn off and my psychotic episode was over. I knew that I probably shouldn't send Marc Finn a fifteen-hundred-word email declaring my love for him. Phew, that was a close one. (Unfortunately, I had an iced coffee two days later and sent it. No, we are not currently dating.)

It was only recently, when I drank Coke Zero every day for a week, didn't sleep, dominated a PowerPoint presentation and then cried while watching *March of the Penguins* shortly afterwards that I came to a realisation. It's not me; it's caffeine. Years of sleepless nights and having my emotions vacillate between feeling on top of the world and actually crying on my kitchen floor, curled into the foetal position, were finally explained. I have traced all of these 'episodes' back to that tiny little ingredient beginning with the letter 'c'. I guess, in a weird way, it's a good thing. I mean, who needs cocaine when there's caffeine? Seems like the US government might need to rethink the War on Drugs.

Don't: Do drugs unless you're good at them, which you probably aren't.

Unlike former president Bill Clinton, I inhaled. And it got awkward. And then I went back and tried to smoke weed about twenty more times. I wanted to see if I could get the hang of being high while appearing somewhat normal, but nope, it got awkward every time.

This is what would happen: I would inform my companions that I didn't smoke pot because I got really weird. They would all laugh and peer-pressure me into 'just having one puff'. Seeing as I tend to abuse things, one puff became three, and Normal Summer became High Summer. High Summer goes back and forth from uncontrollable laughter to intense paranoia. High Summer also gains an insatiable appetite for pizza, ice-cream, Butterfingers, Stouffer's Macaroni and Cheese, Bagel Bites, burritos, chips and salsa, salt and vinegar potato chips, Gatorade and McDonald's. And she wants all of that on top of a Fritos corn chip. Oh, and then she'll wash it down with some prosciutto and Nutella (separately, of course). Come to think of it, I'm really bummed out that I suck at recreational pot smoking. I mean, how could I ever have made it in LA without mastering marijuana? Los Angelinos talk about weed like rich people talk about wine.

Even though I can't hack the green, I did sneak through the metaphorical gateway to new drugs. First stop: psychedelic mushrooms with Brett and his friends, on a Florida beach. I ate them and immediately told Donna. She told me that the next four to eight hours were going to be amazing and to curl up in bed whenever I wanted. And she wasn't kidding; they were amazing. The first five minutes involved a minor freak-out while crouching next to a sand dune. When I looked into the wall of sand, I swore that it was a dark cave, with roots dangling from the ceiling.

After I'd voiced my fear of this horrifying underground world, Brett and his friends came to my side. They mentioned that I just took drugs and needed to be more positive. Together, we left my cave, scooped up some wet sand from the shoreline and began forming sand balls.

Once we shaped them, we began rolling the balls around in the palms of our hands. Within an hour, they were perfectly shaped and hard as cement. Admiring the science that was going on, I decided that I felt safe just as long as I had my ball. Later, I enjoyed watching the moon dance like a strobe light on the waves and practised jumping as the wind blew sheets of sand at my feet. It felt as if the world was flirting with me. With my sand ball in one hand and the wind wrapping around my body, I was blissfully content. Shrooms had done me proud.

Even though I was much better at mushrooms than I was at pot, I didn't want to make a habit of it. The main reason was that I had been told to never look in a mirror while tripping on shrooms. Not that I'm obsessed with myself, but I honestly don't think I could not look in a mirror for six hours. This probably has to do with my addiction to popping zits and digging at blackheads. (Seriously, I once rubbed butter on a zit so that it would get extra-infected.)

In the search for a much more social drug that could also cater to my vanity, I decided to try cocaine. The first time I did a line, I felt focused. It was like I needed to read, write and communicate. I also felt like I had unstoppable diarrhoea. Unlike my friends, who would do coke before going out to bars at night, I loved doing it in the daytime. I would take a bump, clean my room, go for a run and study for an exam.

Cocaine proved to be a very productive drug for me. However, when I would go shopping on coke, it made me quite impulsive. (See: my three-item purchase totalling $580 from a super-cute Boston boutique called LF, and my $2900 wedding dress purchase of 2010.) After getting stuck with that wedding dress (which I didn't actually love, but purely bought because I was 'getting my wedding planned' while on coke), I realised that this was a seriously fucked-up drug. When I confessed to Donna after my wedding that I had been on coke during our shopping trip, she slapped my shoulder and said, 'Summer! I had THIRTY KILOS to lose for your wedding. You had COCAINE and didn't share?' Oh Donna.

Although cocaine was out of my price range, ecstasy was most certainly not. On my twenty-second birthday, my friends and I willingly decided to go to a gay nightclub called Throb in Darwin to see their acclaimed performance of Trannyformers ('You never know what we'll change into next'). What I didn't willingly decide to do was take ecstasy. But, unsurprisingly, I was easily persuaded after a couple of beers. So, when Emily and I went to the bathroom, we didn't protest when our friend Keilon gently slipped a pill into each of our mouths.

The rest of the night was a blast. I was the absolute happiest birthday girl in the world. Until I woke up the next morning. I came to feeling like I had just licked a bowl of bleach and then got in a car accident. My body was lethargic, like I'd been transformed into a slow loris overnight. Regrettably, I started looking through my camera and found a 3:44 video of myself on stage. Apparently, my friends had arranged for the head drag queen to interview me. In this video I was literally licking the air and focusing on nothing in particular. Then I repeated the phrase 'I'm an American stereotype' roughly four times before I realised they were making fun of me. (I swear it was a witty response at the time. But only stated once.)

After I watched this evidence of a drugged-up Summer, I began to recall the few hours after the shameful interview. Emily butt-dialled her new boyfriend while prematurely confessing her love for him to me, and I licked a stripper pole. Then we went home to watch the sunrise from our apartment building's pool. A couple of days later, I got a text message from a number that was saved in my phone as 'Caroline Throb USA'. Apparently, I confessed my love for her while rolling my heart out on E. I love/hate ecstasy. Just like I love/hate tequila.

I think it's safe to conclude that, after nearly ten years of experimenting with drugs, I suck at them. No matter which one of the afore-mentioned substances I consume, I basically become a hysterical, sexually confused, laughing, paranoid dance maniac with a shopping problem. You can see why I just do iced tea and coffee now. Sure, we all know how bad I can get on caffeine. But at least I can balance those out with a glass of red wine. And that's what I call self-control.

A Donnalandish Thought on Snacks:

You don't have to be stoned or pregnant to eat Doritos with caviar.

Do:
Take a
chill pill.

My early twenties brought on an unexpected, irrational anxiety disorder. I think it was a combination of an existential crisis and my age that made me act like a lunatic for a good three years. (And maybe there was a bit of caffeine abuse. And maybe it was partly due to the fact that I have a vagina and am always emotional.) But this disorder was no joke. I started to refuse to drive anyone around because I feared that I would crash and kill us both (or worse: only them). I had nightmares about plummeting to my death in an airplane and absolutely insisted that Donna called me every day, so that I would know she was alive and happy. I also had to make sure that I ran my foot under the extra water that dropped out of the showerhead every time I turned off the shower. For whatever reason, I felt that as long as I did that, all would be well.

Despite not knowing the root of my neurosis, I knew it needed to stop. I couldn't take another panic attack or case of shingles. (By the way, when the doctor told me I had herpes zoster, I freaked out, thinking he meant herpes. Like, sex herpes. Finally, he clarified that it was just the return of my chickenpox. Then he added that I did have an STD ... a Stress Transmitted Disease. He laughed. It wasn't funny.)

After the Shingles Outbreak from Hell, I decided it was time to find my way back to obliviousness. Clearly, my body was telling me to chill the fuck out. I yearned to laugh all day long and only worry about how many scoops of ice-cream I wanted for dinner. But I mostly just wanted to feel comfortable travelling again. I mean, I had moved all the way to Australia to be with Paul. If I didn't get over my irrational fear, I might never be able to fly back to the States to see my friends and family. The thing is, I used to be an awesome flyer. Airports used to be my favourite places to be; there was so much energy created by people from all around the world bustling through them. Not to mention the fact that I thrive on networking and love making a good connection. (No pun intended, but it's amazing.)

At twenty-three, I was still mid–anxiety disorder and not a happy traveller. I was flying from Australia, via Fiji and a bunch of other cities, to Florida with one of my best friends, Molly. I was heading home for a wedding and was incredibly relieved that Molly was going to be on the plane with me. To gear up for the ten-hour journey from Fiji to Los Angeles, I made sure to pack some Ambien and my laptop (loaded with episodes of *Intervention*, *Hoarders* and *I Used To Be Fat*). I also made sure to ask for a window seat so I could pass out against a wall.

Armed with all of my vices, I was finally ready to relax. What I was *not* ready for was to be seated away from Molly and in a seat that was basically on the aisle because of a one-foot gap to the window. With a double whammy like that, I was on the fast track to a blackout sob-fest. It seemed like a good idea to have some wine with dinner and put on a movie before popping a little sleeping pill; it would be the best way to fast-forward through the flight. I narrowed down my cinematic choices to *Soul Surfer: The Bethany Hamilton Movie* and *Justin Bieber: Never Say Never*. I decided to start with Bethany because, up until that point, I wasn't a 'Belieber'.

Midway through the mushy airplane meal (which I secretly enjoyed, but pretended I didn't because I wanted to act grossed out like everyone else), Bethany lost an arm to a shark. The thing was, she had still managed to show more courage than I had at that very moment on the plane. I sobbed dramatically as she got back in the water and learned to surf again. I sobbed even *more* dramatically as her family fought for her. And I damn near lost it as she came back even more triumphant than before. It was at that point I decided to be brave. Time to dry my tears and get to know the boy sitting next to me. After I explained my new love for Bethany Hamilton and how I planned to take up surfing, I learned that he was seventeen and from Newport Beach, California. No, I do not remember his name.

Apparently, in a broken-down-from-*Soul-Surfer*-red-wine-sleeping-pill state, we began chatting about movies. He told me that he and his friends had been in Fiji to film some underwater scenes for a documentary they were making. (So much more productive than I was in high school. They must grow them differently in California.) I'm not sure why the nature movie discussion compelled me to do what I did next, but I told him that he ABSOLUTELY NEEDED to watch *The Wild and Wonderful Whites of West Virginia*. (If you haven't seen this cinematic masterpiece, you need to put down this book and iTunes it right now. Think inbred Americans, drugs, guns and beer. God bless the White family. Yewwwww!)

With that, I handed over my new MacBook Pro and set him up on iTunes Movie Viewer. The next thing I remember was being woken up after landing, the kid placing my laptop in the seat pocket in front of me. He said it was an awesome documentary and absolutely crazy. I was so relieved to be on solid ground that I didn't even have time to think about the fact I had given a seventeen-year-old my laptop for a ten-hour flight. I just hope that he didn't go through my iTunes library. I have everything from Aqua to INXS. I also totally have a file with naked pictures. (I know that I know better, but sometimes you just do it.) I went to the bathroom to freshen up and did my best to remove the red-wine stains from my teeth and lips.

Sadly, Los Angeles was *not* the last stop on my way home. I now had to trek from Los Angeles to Atlanta to Gainesville to Charlotte to Wilmington. This was because I had become completely brain dead when it came to booking flights and paying attention to important dates and times. You see, I originally thought I was going to Gainesville and then driving to Wilmington with Donna for the wedding. But noooooooooo, I booked the wrong day and now had to play catch up. Magically, I made it to Wilmington. But, due to a hurricane, my luggage did not. Also, the wedding had to be moved up to that same day because of crappy weather. So there I was, after forty hours of travel, with only the clothes on my back and the red wine on my teeth. Did I mention I was in a tank top and that all of my armpit hair had grown back in? I was not fresh.

For the wedding, I ended up wearing one of my brother's girlfriend's dresses and managed to look somewhat presentable. As a Category 4 hurricane blew all around us in the awesome harbour ceremony, Marjorie and Jason said, 'I do'. We were then evacuated inland. The entire bridal party decided to continue the celebration in the lobby of a Hampton Inn, since they had a generator. Plenty of pizzas and Coronas later, we all toasted the lovely union and went to bed. (By 'went to bed' I mean that Marjorie and Jason consummated their marriage in the lobby bathroom.)

Since I was safe in the arms of friends and family, I managed to come back down to level-headed Summer for a month. But as my return to Australia approached I became quite distraught. My anxiety started creeping back in, telling me to freak out about flying. I was fine on the trip from Florida to Los Angeles; flying over land doesn't really stress me out. But the whole water thing sure did. I dislike salt water, being cold and man-eating sharks (especially the ones with frickin' laser beams attached to their heads). Maybe it was a mix of *Austin Powers* and *Titanic* that instilled the fear in me. When I was sat next to a nice young English couple for the LA-to-Sydney leg, I was relieved. I told myself that God couldn't possibly kill such a cute couple. (This may seem weird, but I always look for small children on my flights. I like to tell myself that nothing bad would ever happen to them.)

Safely in position next to my nice English couple, I prepared for take-off. Unfortunately, this take-off was MUCH more turbulent than usual, and breathing was becoming hard. I was freaking out. I glanced over at the couple for some support, but they were busy holding hands with each other (so selfish). Who was going to hold *my* hand? No one. I was going to die alone. I quickly popped a sleeping tablet, put my tiny blue airplane blanket over my head and cried. Like, dying geese–style crying. During this period, I kept trying to rationalise the turbulence. *It's just the wind and it will all be better once we reach 37,000 feet.* And it was, of course; after that, the plane became very calm. I, on the other hand, remained restless and completely distraught (you might call it 'mental turbulence'). This seemed like the perfect time to get into the Justin Bieber movie. I needed a distraction, and I needed it now. Plus, I love a good inspiring story about a young Canadian boy finding fame on YouTube.

Surprisingly, this movie actually made me even *more* hysterical than the Bethany Hamilton story, the red wine and the Ambien, *combined*. THIS KID IS AMAZING. I couldn't believe his talent and energy. So now I wanted to take over the world, one tween at a time. *Never Say Never* had just etched out a spot in my top three most influential and inspiring movie star docs of all time. (The other two being *E! True Hollywood Story: Taylor Swift* and *E! True Hollywood Story: Jenna Jameson*. I know these are two very different women, but they are both so driven and talented … in their own ways.)

I got off that plane a new person. I was not only a 'Belieber', but I was also a *believer*. I realised that I could accomplish all of my goals as long as I trusted the world and myself. Justin was so fearless in his gallivanting around the globe, having such a positive effect on so many people. I decided that I would face my fears, write my book and chase after all of my dreams. Never say never. Just like Justin.

Do: Let a celebrity fall in love with you.

With my fear of flying nixed (okay, fine, I discovered Xanax), I flew back to the US in May 2012 to get things ready for our wedding. Since Paul had work, he planned on meeting me that July. I'm never one to be excited about flying to Los Angeles (something about those crushed dreams as a seventeen-year-old). So I was even less excited to have landed at LAX only to be stuck waiting on the sidewalk for my friend Erica and holding two giant bags. Not to mention, I had spilled Pepto-Bismol and cream cheese on my black pants, had failed to brush my teeth and was forming a nice plot of real estate for a rat's nest on the top of my head. Basically, I looked like Britney, circa K-Fed, and smelled like baby vomit. (Something I'm sure she can relate to.)

Plus, it's tough waiting for someone to pick you up when you don't exactly know what car they drive because they tell you to look for the 'black Toyota'. I creepily smiled and jumped up and down at approximately six black Toyotas, which frightened the drivers enough to convince me to give up trying to act enthusiastic. Instead, I resorted to waiting for Erica with a bored frown.

Some time around the twenty-minute mark of my sulking, I looked inside at the baggage carousel and saw what looked like a sculpted wall of flesh gliding through the airport. As my eyes focused, I realised that this mass of human was none other than the Italian supermodel Fabio Lanzoni. His crystalline blue eyes scanned over the common people with their common suitcases as he located his belongings. I imagined a dark leather trunk riding around the conveyor belt, filled with swords, massage oils and a satin robe.

Completely shocked by this celebrity sighting of epic proportions (I mean, this is the guy who has graced hundreds of romance novel covers, took a goose to the face *and* could not believe it was not butter!!!) I called Erica and explained that she needed to arrive, immediately. I *had* to go and take a picture with Fabio but couldn't leave the kerb, as I had my entire life at my feet (at least that's what I think I said in my jumbled, starstruck words). As if the hands of fate were arranging this photo op, Erica pulled up just in time for me to abandon my bags and sprint into the baggage claim.

When I approached Fabio, there were already a couple of people taking pictures with him, so I politely asked if I could do it too. His golden locks were dancing on his shoulders as gracefully as 100,000 Mikhail Baryshnikovs when his eyes locked with mine. Now, not to sound self-absorbed, but I am acutely aware of my ability to make people fall in love with me by holding eye contact for an uncomfortable period of time. It worked with my fiancé and it was clearly working with Fabio. As his blue eyes peered into my soul, my eyes transmitted images of the two of us on a bearskin rug, with a bottle of red wine placed between my thighs (and myself between his thighs, of course).

Knowing that I had him, I switched up my game and decided to play coy. I went to stand next to him for my picture, but kept my distance. He obviously needed me closer and pulled me tight against his chest (his hairless, exposed chest). My face being buried into his magnificent man cleavage, coupled with the overwhelming aroma of Italian supermodel, made me go weak at the knees. (Well played, Fabio.) I gently squeezed his lower back (also hairless, I assume) with my left hand and thanked him for the photo.

Although I was intoxicated by his man scent, I gathered up all of my strength to walk away. Inside, I was telling myself not to lead Fabio on because I have a fiancé. But I looked back and made eye contact AGAIN. Boom. His salamander eyes now transmitted images of us kissing, as a waterfall rained down upon our naked, wanting bodies. I gave him a soft smile and turned to go. That's when I heard it – the gentle strum of a harp. I looked back once more to see Fabio nod. It was like he knew that I couldn't be with him because of my love for another.

I'm not sure what's harder: that we had to let each other go or that I have to live with the fact that I could have had Fabio. He and I may always wonder about the life we could have had together. But, one way or another, we will always remember the naked waterfall in his eyes. No one can take that away from us.

Do: Get hitched.

I got to Megan's house in Park City to begin the wedding countdown. Every now and then I would think about Fabio and what could have been, but then Paul would call and that Australian accent would steal my heart all over again. My wedding planner, Melissa, was a great distraction. Together, we basically took over the wedding world. We ordered a massive white tent, garden roses, baby's breath, burlap runners, seersucker bow ties and mason jars galore! (I swear this wasn't a Southern sorority social–themed wedding.) I didn't know that I had the 'bride gene', but give me a glass of wine, a credit card and Etsy.com and I'm pretty much gone. Surprisingly, I was not drunk when I spent $6000 on renting a handmade barn-wood floor. Nope, that was a brilliant decision made by sober Summer.

Even though I was in Park City three weeks before our wedding to relax and finish last-minute details, I was ridiculously stressed. Almost every day I would find a new reason to have a panic attack, binge-eat a bag of gluten-free cookies (that was all I could find in Megan's pantry) and open a bottle of wine. By the time my wedding came around, I was exactly two pounds heavier and had (what I would say was) cystic acne. Planning a wedding is hard. Even when you have the best wedding planner in the world. Which I did. (Her name is Melissa Hagen.)

For me the stress came from being a host. I was intent on making sure everyone would have a great time. Almost every single one of our guests was from out of town, therefore we had arranged to all go to an outdoor concert at Deer Valley on Wednesday night, a coed bachelorette party on Thursday, groomsmen golf and a bridesmaid brunch on Friday morning, followed by a welcome party that night. Saturday was the big day and, of course, a brunch, hosted by friends, would be on Sunday morning. It's no wonder I was freaking out.

Surprisingly, I was incredibly relaxed on Saturday morning. I had all of my very best friends in the world in my hotel suite. We ate breakfast and began the hair and make-up process. Megan painted my toenails. (It was a feat I was particularly proud of, as it took me months to grow my nails [hands and toes] for our wedding. I am a horrible nail biter. It's actually awkward how many times I had worms as a child from biting my dirty toes. Note to self: go see a counsellor about OCD and nail biting.)

With my non-mutilated toes painted a pretty pink and my hair up in a bun, we put my veil on, zipped up my dress and posed for pictures. Before we knew it, it was almost 4:30 p.m. We quickly opened up my laptop, turned on Photo Booth and Carly Rae Jepsen and immediately did a group dance to 'Call Me Maybe'. The wedding planner came in and witnessed nine girls dancing and singing. She also witnessed a half-naked bride (my dress was hot) and a completely naked maid of honour (Megan). Of course, she let us finish, but after that she put our wedding party in line. Literally and figuratively. (She was like Jennifer Lopez in *The Wedding Planner*, but tinier and louder. This girl could make a puppy be productive.)

I could hear the music begin and off walked the first couple. With only seven sets left to go, I grabbed my bouquet and Donna's arm. She squeezed my hand as we stepped closer to the door. Finally, Melissa cued that it was time for us to go. With my head held high and my pageant smile in place, we walked down the aisle. The minute I saw the guests stand for my arrival, I broke out in hives.

I'm going to be super-straight with you here. Walking down an aisle and getting married is extremely intense. I was so overwhelmed by everyone staring at me that I swear I blacked out and have no idea what happened. I do know that I said yes and was given a beautiful ring. I also think I vowed to love Paul forever. All I can say is, thank goodness for the videographer. With the hard part (saying our vows to only mate with each other until death do us part into a microphone in front of friends and family) over, it was time to celebrate.

Megan made a beautiful speech. Matt, Paul's cousin and best man, made a nice speech as well – if you consider this joke funny: 'Paul and I grew up together and we were always racing each other in life. Let's just hope for Summer's sake, Paul doesn't finish first tonight.'

My guests thought it was hilarious. I know that I should have been more laid-back. (I mean, think about everything I've shared with you thus far.) But for some reason, I couldn't stop blushing at the idea of people thinking about me having sex.

With the speeches over, we moved on to the other standard wedding traditions. I only made one *Human Centipede*[2] joke (during the cake-cutting part). Next, we all happily danced the Hora. (The main reason I wanted to get married was so that I could be raised up in a chair. Okay, fine, and because Paul is the love of my life.) When Men at Work's 'Down Under' came on, all of the Aussies really stepped up their game. They grabbed Melissa's beautiful aspen trees which had been cut to hold place cards and used them as makeshift didgeridoos. (Sorry, Melissa.) And what would a wedding be without 'Shout'? Consider it slayed.

Megan caught the bouquet and another of Paul's aussie friends, Matt, caught the garter. This could not have been more perfect. They are both ginormous hams and immediately began to perform when the DJ put on Celine Dion's 'My Heart Will Go On'. There was spinning, dipping, running, twirling and head-to-head contact. During one very close spin, Megan's lip must have slammed against Matt's

---

2   Actually, before we move on. Have you seen that movie? If you have and we are ever in that situation together, I call dibs on Position A. Just saying.

skull because, sure enough, Megan had blood streaming down her face by the end of the song. I immediately ran over and grabbed a white cloth napkin to catch the blood. We walked into my suite so that she could have a rest and have a nurse survey the damage.

Despite a busted lip and lots of spilled red wine, everyone seemed to have a really nice time. We honeymooned in Wyoming, Virginia, North Carolina, Florida, Massachusetts, Rhode Island, California and Hawaii. Needless to say, when we got back to Mudgee, I stayed in bed for forty-eight hours watching nothing but cold-case reality shows and rom coms. Life was good.

LESSONS I REALLY DID LEARN

When asked as a child, 'What do you want to be when you grow up?' I never hesitated to give a garrulous response. I have always been very analytical and I have very good reasoning (well, Summerlandish reasoning, that is) for all of my hopes, dreams and endeavours.

Here's what I wanted to be, with the corresponding years in which I wanted to be it:

Preschool: Princess

Kindergarten: Actress

1st Grade: The lead cat in the musical *CATS!*

2nd Grade: Teacher

3rd Grade: A prostitute or Playboy bunny

4th Grade: Rapunzel

5th Grade: Housewife

6th Grade: Dancer

7th Grade: Actress

8th Grade: Trophy wife

9th Grade: X-ray technician
10th Grade: Tennis club owner
11th Grade: Gym owner
12th Grade: Actress
University: Marketing professional (aka housewife)

When I was twenty-two, I was a college graduate but definitely not anywhere close to being an American version of Rapunzel who doubled as a Broadway triple-threat talent with her own tennis court, gym and X-ray machine. While I did, at least, have a boyfriend, I definitely wasn't close to being a trophy wife. So, around the zillionth time someone asked me what I wanted to be when I grew up, I casually replied, 'A pharmaceutical rep.' (And no, I had not watched *Love & Other Drugs* yet. If I had, then I would definitely be hawking prescription pills and making sweet love to Jake Gyllenhaal at this very moment.) My questioner, Laura's sister Krista, laughed and said that my choice was boring and that I'd be better suited to being a writer. It wasn't because I'm particularly eloquent, but that I always seem to have a lot of stories.

Maybe she was onto something. So I started writing. And, unless you've flipped to the last chapter in the bookstore to see how it ends, you've read a heap of these stories. Looking back on years of public humiliation, horribly awkward tampon exposures, a ripped bum hole and time in the slammer, I've realised that I truly have learnt a lot about myself.

Some highlights include:

I don't want to be someone with a zodiac tattoo. (Thank you, laser removal surgical centre.)
DIY renovations are not my thing.
No one will buy the cow if you're passing the milk out for free. Even if that cow is super-cute, educated,

funny and a 'strong and independent' woman. (Unless you're the 'exception'. If you don't know what I'm talking about, you need to either read or watch *He's Just Not That Into You*.)

Dressing up as a Playboy bunny for Halloween when you're eight may be frowned upon.

Pedicure beads will give you thrush if you use them as bath beads. The following other things will also lead to thrush: antibiotics, polyester pants, vaseline and working as a waitress in a tropical climate.

No amount of *Intervention* or *Hoarders* re-runs will satiate my need for A&E (the TV network, that is).

If you're reading this and you bought it in a bookstore or downloaded it from Amazon, then I guess I'm a writer. But who knows what will happen over the next few years? If it's exciting, I'll write another book. If I'm in jail, well, fuck. If I'm a mom, then maybe I'll be on a reality show as a stage mother. Who knows? I just hope the next twenty-five years are as fun as my first twenty-five.

EPILOGUE

In February 2013 I decided to join the cause FebFast and go alcohol-free for twenty-eight days (thank goodness it wasn't a leap year) to raise money for programs that help young people and families who are tackling serious alcohol and drug issues, because:

1. I liked the cause.

2. I wanted to detox and feel great. (Plus, it was my chance to pretend to be just like Sandra Bullock in *28 Days*.)

Expecting to become a new person with sixpack abs and a clear mind, I was stunned when, instead, I woke up every morning feeling extremely hung-over. And it wasn't just in the mornings. I literally wanted to puke all day, every day. I figured my body must be upset from not getting red wine and hard cider. (Not that I feel like my alcohol intake is that much, but I watch *Intervention* so I know that withdrawal can be a huge symptom of addiction.) Was my body an alcoholic and physically addicted to booze?

Before I made a decision to check into rehab, I decided to take a pregnancy test. I peed on the strip and boom, straight away, two lines. Cue: Jumping up and down with a pee stick and extreme fear all at once. Now, this wasn't technically an unplanned pregnancy. Paul and I'd decided to 'try' one night while drinking white wine. Guess it worked!

I immediately called Donna. We both gushed over the fact that my body was now officially a baby-making factory. I thanked her for making me feel so loved and for telling me that I could be anything I wanted to be, because now I was a happily married published author with a little human on the way. I also told her that I hoped I was half as amazing a mom as she was. She laughed and said that I would definitely be a 'cool mom'. (I just hope my kids know that their Granddonna is responsible for my weirdness and the fact that they will get to go to summer camp every year, dress up as whatever they want for Halloween and eat filet mignon for breakfast if they please.)

When I hung up the phone, I took a deep breath. My emotions were going back and forth between joy, fear, excitement and stress. I mean, this book was just about to be released! But then I realised that this was exactly something I would do. It's just so Summerlandish. (And if Jessica Simpson can promote a billion-dollar fashion line with back-to-back pregnancies, I think I can make this work.) I mean, I've already blown out my anus jumping off a cliff. I think I can handle childbirth.

Whether or not my vagina can will be another story.

ACKNOWLEDGEMENTS

First of all, I'd like to thank Donna for being Donna. (I am so glad you made me.)

I'd also like to thank:

Laura and Krista Hershey for telling me to be a writer.

Rose, Ali, Jeff, Lauren and Toonie for being the best editors in the world.

Emily and Molly for their amazing friendships, design and marketing knowledge. You two have made *Summerlandish* what it is today. I feel like we are doing Emerson College proud!

Megan for being Megan. (You are my childhood.)

If it weren't for David Meerman Scott's countless helpful emails, you probably wouldn't be reading this book right now. And, obviously, if it weren't for Rose and Hardie Grant, you wouldn't be holding this book right now.

Most of all I want to thank my friends and family for making these memories with me. Without you, I wouldn't have had so many chances to embarrass myself. I should also thank Paul for supporting me through this journey and letting me publish all my dirty laundry for the world (and his family) to see. You're my favourite memory.

And to my unborn child: If this book gets you bullied at school, just remember, those kids suck and life will get better! And if it doesn't – write about it and laugh it off.